It takes more than semen to get a cow pregnant. It takes a <u>trusted</u> team.

For decades, producers have trusted Select Sires to provide highly fertile semen from bulls that transmit both production and type. Today, leading producers involve Select Sires representatives as trusted members of their team.

It's tough to successfully manage the many variables that determine whether your cows become pregnant with high-value calves. That's why more producers are including local Select Sires representatives on their management teams. Select's representatives have the expertise to help with reproductive troubleshooting, estrus-synchronization programs, A.I. training and professional technician service.

Rather than depending on a one-size-fits-all reproductive system, Select Sires offers a portfolio of reproductive solutions that can be tailored to meet your individual herd's needs. Ask your Select Sires representative about reproductive solutions for your herd.

Reproductive Solutions™

SELECT SIRES

Tel. (614) 873-4683
Fax (614) 873-5751
www.selectsires.com

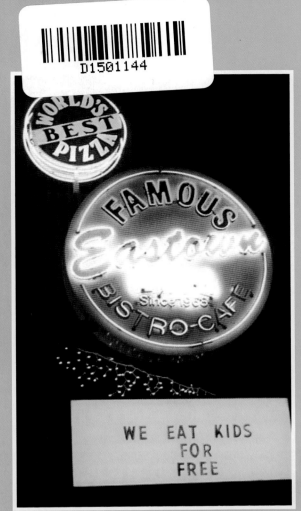

WORLD'S BEST PIZZA

FAMOUS Eastown Since 1963 BISTRO-CAFE

WE EAT KIDS
FOR
FREE

KLEINS
FUNERAL HOME | SUPER MARKET
Serving Magnolia 60 Years

ANY PERSONS (EXCEPT PLAYERS)
CAUGHT COLLECTING GOLF BALLS
ON THIS COURSE WILL BE
PROSECUTED AND HAVE THEIR
BALLS REMOVED

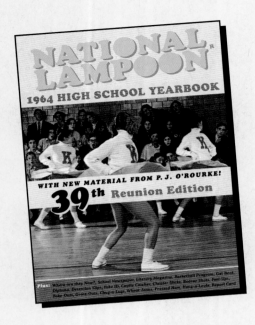

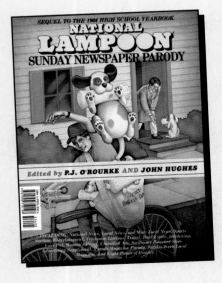

NATIONAL LAMPOON · 10850 WILSHIRE BOULEVARD · LOS ANGELES · CA 90024 · USA

www.NATIONALLAMPOON.com

RUGGED LAND · 401 WEST STREET · SECOND FLOOR · NEW YORK CITY · NY 10014 · USA

RuggedLand

Published by Rugged Land, LLC

276 CANAL STREET • FIFTH FLOOR • NEW YORK CITY • NY 10013 • USA
RUGGED LAND and colophon are trademarks of Rugged Land, LLC.
NATIONAL LAMPOON and colophon are trademarks of National Lampoon.

PUBLISHER'S CATALOGING-IN-PUBLICATION DATA
(Provided by Quality Books, Inc.)

National lampoon's big book of love / edited by Scott
Rubin, Sean Crespo, and Mason Brown.
p. cm.
ISBN 1-59071-059-2

1. Love--Humor. 2. United States--Social life and customs--1971---Humor.
3. American wit and humor. I. Rubin, Scott. II. Crespo,
Sean. III. Brown, Mason.
IV. Title: Big book of love. V. Title: National lampoon.

PN6231.L6N38 2004   818'.602
                           QBI03-700687

RUGGED LAND WEBSITE ADDRESS:WWW.RUGGEDLAND.COM

FIRST RUGGED LAND TRADE
1   3   5   7   9   10   8   6   4   2

NATIONAL LAMPOON's ®

BIG BOOK OF TRUE FACTS

Editor in Chief: Scott Rubin

Art Direction: MoDMaN

Compiled by: Jay Naughton and Tom Snyders

Edited by: Scott Rubin

Page Layout and Design: Jay Naughton

Editorial Assistant: Kim Thompson

Cover Photo of Tom Snyders: Roy Katalan

Cairo Bus Plunge Kills 15

CAIRO, June 27 (Reuters) — Fifteen persons were killed and 17 injured today when a truck plunged into a canal near the Nile River after the driver had swerved to avoid another vehicle.

Ecuador Bus Plunge Kills 19

QUITO, Ecuador, Aug. 28 (Reuters) — Nineteen people were killed and five seriously injured when a crowded bus plunged down a 150-foot ravine in northern Ecuador last night, the police said today. The dead, they said, included an American couple, identified as Thomas and Elsy O'Kelly.

Afghan Bus Plunge Kills 21

KABUL, Afghanistan, May 11 (AP)—Twenty-one persons were killed and six injured when a bus plunged into an irrigation canal in Lashkargah, western Afghanistan, the police reported. They attributed the accident to careless driving.

Chilean Bus Plunge Kills 13

OSORNO, Chile, March 20 (UPI)—Thirteen persons were killed and 34 injured when a bus with an inexperienced driver at the wheel plunged off a mountain road at Puyehue, near the Argentine border 625 miles south of Santiago, the police said today.

35 Injured in Bus Plunge

MARKTHEIDENFELD, West Germany, April 20 (UPI)—At least 35 persons were injured, 10 o fthem seriously, when a bus filled with 52 members of a pensioners club went down an embankment and overturned, the police said today.

Bus Plunge in India Kills 7

NEW DELHI, Dec. 27 (UPI)— Seven policemen were killed and 24 others were injured when a police truck carrying them plunged into a canal near Arrah in the northeastern state of Bihar, the Press Trust of India reported today. The agency said the policemen were on their way to target practice.

Bus Plunge Kills 14 in India

NEW DELHI, July 27 (UPI) — A bus plunged into a 100-foot gorge near a Himalayan hill station at Simla, 250 miles north of here, yesterday killing 14 persons and injuring 45 others, the Press Trust of India reported today.

Six Killed in Bus Plunge

SARAGOSSA, Spain, Dec. 19 (Reuters) — A bus carrying about 50 Spanish workers and their families home for Christmas from West Germany and Switzerland plunged off a bridge into the Ebro River here early today. At least six persons were killed and about 40 were injured. Most of the passengers escaped through a rear exit.

Mexican Bus Plunge Kills 8

PALMAR CHICO, Mexico Oct. 27 (UPI)—Eight persons died of injuries suffered when a bus plunged off a wet road into a 400-foot-deep gully, the police reported. The police said the bus had been overloaded, carrying more than 50 passengers.

12 Die in Ceylon Bus Plunge

COLOMBO, Ceylon, Sept. 12 (AP) — A bus plunged down a 100-foot precipice today at Agraptatana, killing 12 persons and injuring 50.

Bus Plunge in Brazil Kills 30

BELEM, Brazil, July 19 (UPI) —Thirty persons were killed yesterday when a bus fell off a ferry ramp into the Capim River, and an unknown number are missing, the police said to-ay. The accident occurred at São Domingos, 250 miles southeast of this Amazon delta port.

Colombia Bus Plunge Kills 12

BOGOTA, Colombia, April 11 (Reuters)—Twelve people died and 15 were injured when a bus plunged nearly 500 feet down a ravine outside Linares, near the Ecuadorean frontier, it was reported here today.

Compiled from the New York Times over a surprisingly short period of time.

TRUE rules

TRUE leadership

It had been thought that following the death of Walt Disney, the atmosphere at the Disney studios in Hollywood would ease somewhat, but Mr. Disney had prepared a method of retaining some postmortem control.

About a year after his death, a memo was sent to all key department heads at the studio instructing them to attend a special screening in one of the projection rooms. When the executives entered the room, they were told to seat themselves accord- ing to the name cards arranged around the room.

The lights dimmed, the curtains were drawn open, and a motion picture of Disney sitting behind his desk came on. He addressed every one of them by name, pointing and speaking directly to each one in turn, and demanding an account of the progress of their projects. He then outlined what he expected of each of them, and when he finished, he told them they would be seeing him again.
Santa Monica Evening Outlook

TRUE tysonosity

Albert Collins, a sixty-six-year-old apartment manager at 1214 Pennsylvania St., in Kansas City, went to the apartment of Hans J. Von Peshke, thirty-three, to complain about noise coming from his apartment.

According to police, Collins told Von Peshke that he had had "an earful" of the noise he had been making.

Von Peshke reportedly told Collins he would "fix it," and then seized Collins and bit off the upper part of his ear.

Kansas City Star

TRUE mortality

The town of Walled Lake, Michigan, had been having difficulty selling city cemetery plots, and at the urging of mayor Bill Roberts, the city council decided to pass a resolution striking down a previous resolution which said that a person had to be dead to purchase a plot.

"That could be part of the reason they're not selling too well," commented the mayor. *Walled Lake Spiral Column*

TRUE fission

TRUE

The corporation which is the principal producer of fuel for atomic power plants in Germany is named Nukem.
Forbes

TRUE winner

Ian Moor, 31, signed up for a Special Olympics contest in York, England, called the National Paraplegic Championships. He arrived in a hand-operated car, hoisted himself into his wheelchair, entered several field events, and won first prize in the wheelchair discus throw.

Moor was disqualified, however, after neighbors saw a picture of him in the paper holding the winning ribbon. They recognized Moor as the man who delivered the paper. National Paraplegic Championships officials said they had no idea Moor is a perfectly healthy individual who walks a mail route for a living.

When questioned about the charade, Moor announced, "It's all a mistake. I'm sick."

UPI

TRUE medicine

David Sherer of Ligonier, Indiana, while recovering from an illness, fell off the side of his bed and wedged his head in a plastic wastebasket.

He was found dead of suffocation a short time later.

AP

MEAT RAFFLE
SATURDAY
1:30
ALL WELC

Amigone
Funeral Home
569

HICKY WICKY
ROOTY TOOTY
CAR WASH

A Brazilian man was waiting for his six-year-old son to cross a street in a small town near Rio de Janeiro when a car struck the boy and killed him. Several hours later, the grieving, raging father returned to the site of the accident, where he began hurling rocks at every passing vehicle. Three angered motorists eventually stopped, crushed him to death with boulders, and drove away.

Agence France Presse

URINATING IN PUBLIC IS A VIOLATION OF ARS.13-2904

TRUE rules

TRUE dessert

Robert C. H. Hershey, an employee at the Pepperidge Farm plant in Downingtown, Pennsylvania, was killed when he fell into a vat of chocolate.

Hershey apparently removed the cover of an automatic chocolate mixing tub, then fell in. A local rescue squad had to cut through the machine's steel housing to retrieve his body.

Baltimore Sun

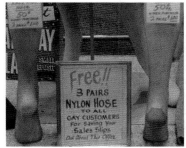

TRUE matrimony

In 1956, a Parisian night watchman named Noel Carriou became enraged when his wife cooked a roast too rare and threw her out of bed in the middle of the night. Mme. Carriou suffered a broken neck and died. He was sentenced to twelve years at hard labor. Released after seven years because of good behavior, he remarried. Unfortunately, his second wife, Clemence, shared his first wife's fatal lack of cooking skill. After being served a burnt roast, M. Carriou exclaimed, "You cook like a Nazi," and stabbed her to death.

M. Carriou has been sentenced to another eight years in prison.
San Francisco Chronicle

TRUE opinion

A woman was sunbathing in her backyard in Saint Louis when Henry Polcynski, a thirty-eight-year-old neighbor, suddenly appeared with a hammer and beat her severely around the head and upper body while shouting, "I don't like sunbathers!"

After his arrest, Polcynski added, in a single, one-sentence statement to police, "The metric system angers me."
UPI

禁止進入事項

一、攜帶家犬牲畜危險品者
二、傳染病精神病患者
三、未身露體衣履不整者
四、小販兜售商品者

THOSE WHO ARE NOT WELCOME AS FOLLOWS:

1. DOMESTIC ANIMALS AND DANGEROUS GOODS CARRIERS.
2. INFECTIOUS AND ABNORMAL-MINDED INVALIDS.
3. STARK NAKED, BARE-FOOTED, AND RAGGED-CLOTHED.
4. PEDDLERS AND HAWKERS.

• LIVES OF THE GREAT •

SIGMUND FREUD (1856-1939)

"THE CREATOR AND FOUNDER OF PSYCHOANALYSIS."
IN THE EARLY 1900s, FREUD WAS LOOKED ON AS A PERVERT WHO ADVOCATED "FREE LOVE AND A RELAPSE INTO SAVAGERY."

FREUD WAS AFRAID OF TRAINS AND HATED MUSIC BUT LOVED CIGARS. HE SMOKED TWENTY OR MORE A DAY.

IN ONE OF THE MORE THAN 1500 LOVE LETTERS HE WROTE TO HIS FIANCÉE, MARTHA BERNAYS, FREUD WROTE: "...YOU SHALL SEE WHO IS STRONGER, A GENTLE LITTLE GIRL WHO DOESN'T EAT ENOUGH, OR A BIG WILD MAN WITH COCAINE IN HIS BODY."

ONCE, ANGRY WITH HIS PARENTS, YOUNG SIGMUND WALKED INTO THEIR ROOM AND URINATED ON THE FLOOR.

FREUD SPENT HIS TWENTY-FOURTH BIRTHDAY IN JAIL FOR BEING AWOL FROM HIS AUSTRIAN ARMY UNIT. IT WAS HIS EIGHTH OFFENCE.

L. Aries

TRUE . . . huh ?

TRUE cripple

Albert Stewart, a twenty-three-year-old paraplegic, was making conversation at a party on the South Side of Chicago when Kelvin Adams interrupted him by asking, "What?" Stewart shouted back, "Don't say 'what' to me," drew a pistol from beneath his paralyzed legs, and shot Adams dead. Stewart then forced another guest to help him maneuver his motorized wheelchair down a flight of stairs, and sped away.

The Daily Californian

TRUE-o-rama

From a National Aeronautics and Space Administration instruction:

The program executed an execute instruction which tried to execute another execute. Check for program instruction modification.

TRUE government

From the Federal Register:

For a position to be considered eligible employment under this part, it must be one for which the employer normally has compensated other persons not employed under this part. If no other person has held or is holding that position for that employer, it is one for which most other employers would normally compensate persons holding that position.

From a Department of Energy memorandum:

If after being notified of early dismissal, the employee departs on annual leave prior to the time set for dismissal, leave is charged from the time of departure until the time set for dismissal. If a dismissal time is set before an employee on leave can report for duty, leave is charged up to the dismissal time.

TRUE justice

Charles V. Probert, forty-two, ran afoul of the Michigan Judicial Tenure Board while he was serving as a municipal judge in Wyoming, Michigan. The board turned up a long list of misconduct and ultimately found that Probert was "flagrantly dishonest."

Wyoming's voters then turned down the judge's reelection bid, so he tried to commit suicide with a .25 caliber pistol. Probert didn't die, but he did blow out his right eye in the attempt.

Now he has sued for $50,000 plus $200 a week for life under Michigan's workmen's compensation laws. The former judge claims his new disability is job-related.
Detroit News

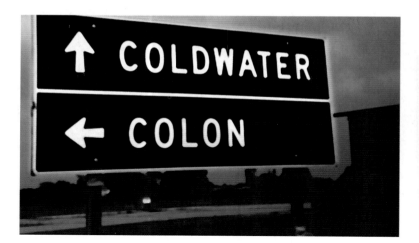

Two fishermen who lost their boat in a storm near the Philippines claimed they survived four days at sea by eating a T-shirt.
Philadelphia Inquirer

A giant shark that was scheduled to be a delicacy in a fish market in Manila suddenly discouraged prospective buyers when a woman's head popped out of the fish's belly as it was being cut open. The shark was of the hammerhead variety and weighed about a ton. It had been captured by five fishermen of Cebu Province.

Deeper in the eighteen-foot-long beast's belly were human limbs and the remains of what looked like a dog.
New York Post

In Toronto, one man was stabbed and police reinforcements were called out to restore order after violence broke out at a Tupperware party.
CP

TRUE wager

In a Sydney, Australia, suburb, a twenty-five-year-old Canberra man bet a friend $600 that he could beat him to the street from an eighth-floor apartment. While his friend ran for the stairway, the man jumped off the balcony to his death.

New Zealand Press Association

The owners of a wildlife preserve in Winston, Oregon are desperately searching for a female companion for George, a two-humped camel who is so sexually frustrated that he has tried to mate with a fifteen-passenger minibus.

"He works up a good frothing at the mouth and makes clumsy, lunging, drooling passes at the park's minibus every time it passes through his territory," says an official of Wildlife Safari, George's home.

George is twenty-seven years old, the equivalent of about ninety human years.

Morristown, N.J. Daily Record

TRUE spin

In an inspired burst of euphemism following a cave-in at one of its mines, DeWitt W. Buchanan, president of the Old Ben Coal Corporation, announced in late October that its King Station coal mine at King Station, Ind., was idled due to "the roof and floor having come together."

Wall St. Journal

TRUE crime

Two hold-up-men drove into a Jack-in-the-Box drive through hamburger stand in Los Angeles and ordered two soft drinks to go. Then, according to the police, one of them left the car and approached Cordia Beverly Downs, eighteen, who was manning the take-out window.

"Give me all your money, and if you think I'm kidding, in about two minutes I'll show you that I'm not," he told her.

Miss Downs handed him a fistful of one dollar bills and watched as the man got back into the car.

He started the engine with some difficulty, and then, as the two men tried to drive away, the car stalled and wouldn't start up again.

The driver got back out, walked up to the counter, and handed back the money.

"Take your money back," he said, "and please don't say anything about this to anyone."

The last Miss Downs saw of them, the two suspects were pushing their car westbound along Fourth Street.

New York Times

•LIVES OF THE GREAT•

CHARLES De GAULLE   (1890-1970)

"[HE IS] THE DULLEST DINNER COMPANION
I EVER MET." - COUNT ALEXANDER DE
STE. PHALLE.
"I AM FRANCE." - CHARLES De GAULLE.

CAPTURED BY THE
GERMANS IN WORLD
WAR I, DE GAULLE
BECAME FAMOUS
FOR HIS INSANE
ESCAPE ATTEMPTS.
HE ONCE TRIED TO
FAKE JAUNDICE BY
TAKING A POTION
TO MAKE HIS SKIN
TURN YELLOW - IT
TURNED HIM ORANGE
INSTEAD. HE SEWED
HIMSELF A GERMAN
UNIFORM, BUT WAS
CAUGHT WHEN
GUARDS NOTICED
THE SLEEVES CAME
TO HIS ELBOWS.

WHEN PLAYING
ARMY AS A CHILD,
DE GAULLE WOULD
BEAT HIS
BROTHERS
SEVERELY
WHEN THEY
REFUSED TO
SWALLOW HIS
SECRET
MESSAGES.

WHILE
PREMIER,
DE GAULLE WOULD
DISMISS JUDGES
FOR NOT GIVING THE DEATH
PENALTY TO PERSONS WHO
TRIED TO ASSASSINATE HIM.

TACTICS FROM
DE GAULLE'S
15 CENT BOOK, EDGE
OF THE SWORD,
WERE USED
EXTENSIVELY BY
THE GERMANS
TO OVERRUN
FRANCE.

TRUE policy

A twenty-three-year-old man was arrested in Columbus, Ohio, after he allegedly stole a pair of eyeglasses from a female pedestrian. An ophthalmic motive was ruled out when police searched the suspect's home and discovered eighty additional pairs of women's corrective lenses, which he had been in the process of eating.
Columbus Citizen Journal

TRUE government

An Iowa legislator introduced a resolution that would designate polyester the official state fiber. The proposal followed an unsuccessful attempt to name the ladybug Iowa's official bug (voted down in the state senate after approval by the legislature) and earlier legislation declaring Iowa's official rock to be the geode.

According to geologists, geodes are not even rocks.
Houston Chronicle

TRUE sanity

James Morgan, Sr., of California has a wife, two sons, and a daughter. His wife is in a hospital suffering from cancer. His daughter is confined to another hospital where she is being treated for leukemia. Morgan was riding with his deaf-mute son, James, Jr., to visit his other son, in a third hospital recovering from burns over 80 percent of his body when their car smashed into a telephone pole. James, Jr., was admitted to a hospital with a brain concussion. Mr. Morgan subsequently committed himself to a psychiatric hospital, with the explanation, "I'm going crazy."

LA Herald Examiner

TRUE advertisement

TRUE politics

L.D. Knox had his name legally changed to None of the Above, then attempted to enter a gubernatorial primary in Louisiana. Secretary of State Paul Hardy, also running for governor, refused to place Knox's new name on the ballot, claiming it was "deceptive." None of the Above subsequently asked a federal court to overrule Hardy, on grounds he is being discriminated against because of culture and lack of money. None of the Above said he "wants the voters to have a chance to reject all the other candidates." *UPI*

TRUE negativity

TRUE crime

A gang of vandals broke into a school in Quimper, France, and wrecked four class-rooms. Furniture was overturned, cabinets ransacked, equipment destroyed, and walls and floors spattered with ink. A dove and three Australian parakeets were killed and plucked, and three other birds were smeared with paint. Police identified four suspects, ranging in age from three to six years old.

The children had been reported missing by their parents the night of the crime.
AP

TRUE reasoning

Angry bus patrons in the Midlands of England complained to bus company officials when drivers repeatedly failed to stop and pick them up. They claimed operators would sometimes smile and wave as they drove by. In defense, the company noted, "It is impossible for the drivers to keep their timetable if they have to stop for passengers."
Campus Life

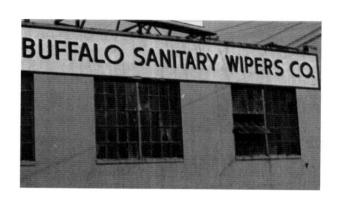

When Mary Wolfe, a sixty-two-year-old arthritic living in Lakeside, Ohio, offered to donate her body to the Medical College of Ohio at Toledo, an official replied that she would have to pay the school to take it.

"Though the donation of one's body to medical education is an act of selfless concern," the official wrote, "budgetary stringencies oblige the college to request a modest sixty dollar fee of each donor."

Ms. Wolfe was also instructed to "make provision for" her own transportation. *AP*

TRUE crime

An unknown man smashed a window at Roger Smith's house in Watsonville, California, entered the home, made Smith's bed, and fled.
UPI

TRUE gourmet

Charles Chamness entered a Sambos restaurant in Tucson, Arizona, and ordered a patty melt, fries, and coffee. When the waitress brought his coffee, Chamness emptied a bottle of Tabasco sauce into it, then dipped two napkins in the cup and swallowed them. He was arrested a short time later for refusing to pay for the patty melt and fries, neither of which he ate.
Tucson Citizen

LIVES OF THE GREAT

JOHN D. ROCKEFELLER 1839-1937

JOHN D., FOUNDER OF THE ROCKEFELLER FORTUNE, CREATED ITS CORNERSTONE, THE STANDARD OIL TRUST, BY SYSTEMATICALLY DESTROYING ALL COMPETITION. HE SAID OF HIS BUSINESS METHODS, "I HAD OUR PLAN CLEARLY IN MIND. IT WAS RIGHT. I KNEW IT AS A MATTER OF CONSCIENCE. IT WAS RIGHT BETWEEN ME AND MY GOD."

EACH YEAR, ROCKEFELLER GAVE HIS GROUNDS KEEPERS A FIVE DOLLAR CHRISTMAS BONUS, THEN DOCKED THEM FIVE DOLLARS FOR TAKING THE DAY OFF.

ROCKEFELLER'S PHILANTHROPY TOOK MANY FORMS. HE MADE HIS EMPLOYEES WORK ON LABOR DAY, EXPLAINING THAT, "INSTEAD OF SPENDING MONEY ON AMUSEMENTS, MY EMPLOYEES WILL BE GIVEN AN OPPORTUNITY TO ADD TO THEIR SAVINGS."

ROCKEFELLER OFTEN GAVE MONEY TO PEOPLE ON THE STREET, A NICKEL FOR CHILDREN AND A SHINY NEW DIME FOR ADULTS. CROWDS SOMETIMES FLOCKED AROUND HIM, ONLY TO DISCOVER THAT HE WAS CHEERFULLY DISTRIBUTING HORSE CHESTNUTS.

THE AGING ROCKEFELLER, IN ANTICIPATION OF HIS DECLINE, HAD HOSPITALS BUILT IN ALL OF HIS HOMES, AND REPORTEDLY HIRED YOUNG MOTHERS TO BREAST-FEED HIM. HE LIVED TO BE ALMOST NINETY-NINE.

TRUE road hazard

PARKING LOT FOR...
HAFEMEISTER'S
FUNERAL HOME
AND
FURNITURE STORE
FOR OVERNIGHT PARKING
PLEASE ASK THE MANAGEMENT

McGEE
LAUNDRY
FAXING
NOTARY
PUBLIC

FAST BREAK DELI
&
FUNERAL PARKING
· ONLY ·
VIOLATORS WILL BE TOWED

AERODYNAMIC
STYLING KITS

SECURITY DEVICES

BRAS

MORTUARY
AFFAIRS
&
FOOD SERVICE
· SVCS. BR. · DOL. PSF ·

Pees HOT
FISH
& WELDING SERVICE

BIG DADDY'S
RECORDS & GROCERIES
SEPTIC TANK REPAIR
920·0370

RON'S GUNS AND COMPUTERS

TRUE variety

RABBITS FOR SALE
BRICKS

BEER
FOOD
WINE
AMMO

PET SHOP
CHINESE FOOD

AVES Wisconsin's Finest
TAXIDERMY & CHEESE

MINNOWS
CRAWDADS
WORMS
SNACKS

Cabbages & Condoms
THAI CUISINE   RESTAURANT
ห้องอาหารซี.แอนด์ซี.
OPEN DAILY 11.00 AM-10.00 PM

Pianos·Organs
Musical Instruments
SEMI AUTO RIFLES
AND PIANOS ON SALE

TV SERVICE and
SOCCER SUPPLIES
Tony's TV & SOCCER SUPPLIES
NOW OPEN

more TRUE variety

TRUE government

In a bid for support from the eighteen members of the local town council of Otsu, Japan, Tsutomu Jodai, a candidate for mayor, said he was "earnest and determined enough to stake my life," then pulled out a knife, put his left hand on a table, and cut off his little finger.

"This is to prove my intentions are honorable and I stand by them as a man," said Mr. Jodai.
New York Times

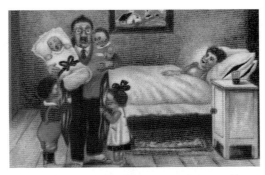 

TRUE mexican postcards

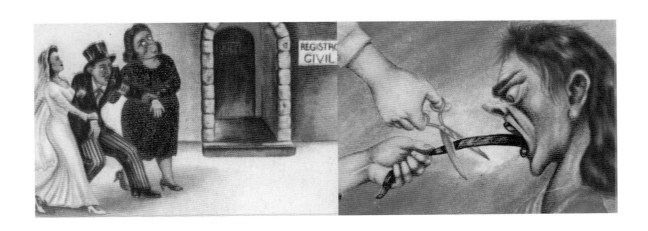

TRUE crime

It took seventy Tokyo police to subdue ten drunken members of a Japanese college judo team as they rampaged through a downtown city street. During the melee, the athletes assaulted three workmen for "glaring" at them, and battered a twenty-four-year-old restaurant cook because he wore an unattractive Hawaiian shirt.
Honolulu Advertiser

TRUE crime

A Toronto gas-station cashier had no trouble identifying a robber for police even though the holdup man had worn a pair of women's shorts over his head as a disguise. The thief, who later admitted that his mind was "clouded" by intoxicants, had stuck his face through one of the leg holes so he could see.

Toronto Star

When a domestic Nigeria Airways flight turned out to be overbooked by three seats Nigerian officials "asked the passengers to run twice around the plane, with the fastest qualifying for seats."
Executive Travel Magazine

TRUE marketing

TRUE verdict

Orange County, California, Superior Court has ordered a local hospital to pay $250,000 to a Huntington Beach woman who suffered "permanent lung damage following an improperly administered enema."
Los Angeles Herald Examiner

The two-year-old daughter of Bapusnheb Kukulwar of Yavatmal, India, was playing in the courtyard of her house when she spotted a black cobra close by. Her parents were watching when the little girl grabbed the snake and instinctively put it in her mouth.

They rushed to take the deadly snake from her, but the girl had already bitten the reptile to death.
Hindustan Times

TRUE reptiles

According to police in Blackfoot, Idaho, Paul Galegos was admitted to a hospital for snakebite treatment after he tried to get a rattlesnake to drink from a beer can. The snake belonged to a friend of Galegos's and had been released in the back of a pickup truck.

There, Galegos had tapped the snake on the head with one hand while he held the can of beer in front of it with the other. Then, police say, he tried to pour the beer down the snake's throat. That's when the rattler bit him on the thumb.
UPI

TRUE honor

A US Navy honor guard on hand for a sea burial aboard the guided-missile destroyer *Farragut* was ordered to fire at the coffin which floated rather than sank when it was dropped into the ocean. The three riflemen fired over 200 shots, finally blowing out the bottom of the coffin and sinking it.

According to a navy spokesman, no violations of regulations were involved in the incident because there are no written instructions on what to do in such circumstances.
AP

LIVES OF THE GREAT

GEORGE HERMAN "BABE" RUTH
(1895 - 1948)

THE "BABE" ROSE FROM AN IMPOVERISHED CHILDHOOD ON THE BALTIMORE WATERFRONT TO BECOME BASEBALL'S LEGENDARY "SULTAN OF SWAT." SPORTSWRITER DICK SCHAAP FELT THAT HE "EMBODIED ALL THAT WAS GOOD IN PRO SPORTS AND MOST OF WHAT WAS BAD," AND NEW YORK'S MAYOR JIMMY WALKER CALLED HIM "A GREAT ATHLETE AND A GREAT FOOL."

THE PRESS DUTIFULLY ATTRIBUTED RUTH'S 1935 SPRING TRAINING COLLAPSE TO "INTESTINAL PROBLEMS." HE WAS IN FACT SUFFERING FROM AN ADVANCED CASE OF SYPHILIS.

RUTH'S NOISY FONDNESS FOR PROSTITUTES AND HIS DISREGARD FOR PERSONAL HYGIENE (HE SELDOM USED A TOOTHBRUSH OR FLUSHED A TOILET) MADE HIM A VERY UN-POPULAR ROOMMATE AT AWAY GAMES.

RUTH'S MIDNIGHT SNACKS USUALLY RAN TO SIX OR SEVEN SANDWICHES WITH THE SAME NUMBER OF BEERS OR SODAS, AND HIS PREGAME MEALS OFTEN CONSISTED OF TRIPLE PORTIONS OF FOOD, WASHED DOWN WITH A QUART OF ORANGE JUICE AND A FIFTH OF GIN.

WHILE ON A WINTER BURLESQUE/ PUBLICITY TOUR, THE BABE WAS SAID TO HAVE CLOSETED HIMSELF IN HOTEL ROOMS WITH AS MANY AS TWELVE PROS-TITUTES AT A TIME, EMERGING ONLY FOR HIS NIGHTLY STAGE APPEARANCE.

TRUE contradiction

TRUE protests...

...or not

In a serious security leak, a man urinated on the Tomb of the Unknown Soldier at the Arc de Triomphe in Paris, putting out the eternal flame. The incident took place only hours after the Chancellor of West Germany laid a wreath at the spot.

French police said the man, a thirty-two-year-old Algerian, was apparently mentally unstable and did not seem to be protesting the visit of the German leader.

University of Michigan Daily

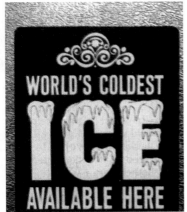

TRUE religion

A religious sect has registered for tax-exempt status in Utah: the Church of Jayne Mansfield of the New Atomic Age. Its founders say the church's doctrine is premised on their belief that "present laws of physics are passing away"
Atlanta Constitution

TRUE rules

New York City Fire Department regulations prohibit firemen from giving mouth-to-mouth resuscitation to animals.
Philadelphia Evening Bulletin

TRUE creativity

In, an attempt to boost morale, the Army Materiel Command (AMC) held a contest to name its new national headquarters building. More than five hundred names were sent in and duly considered by the AMC's official Contest Committee to Name the New Building.

The winning name, submitted by Francis Sikorski, a civilian employee, was "The AMC Building."
Daily Iowan

TRUE demo

The Burke, Virginia, Volunteer Fire Department bought a six-thousand-dollar cutting tool used to dissect wrecked cars with people trapped inside them, and decided to stage a demonstration for the community.

Forty persons watched two firemen sever the doors from a 1969 Buick, slice off its steering wheel, knock out the windows, and pull the steering column out through the windshield.

Then someone shouted, "Hey, what are you doing?" The firemen had attacked the wrong car. The 1969 Buick belonged to the chief of the fire department.
AP

TRUE slacking

TRUE sign-off

An Oregon radio listener, who was first annoyed, then concerned when no one changed the record after the music finished, telephoned the studio to complain. When he got no answer, he called the police.

When the Oregon City police arrived at the KYXI studio, they found that the disk jockey, Michael David Roberts, twenty-two, had committed suicide by hanging himself with a telephone cord.

The last record Roberts had played? "Softly as I Leave You."

Durham Morning Herald

TRUE fink

Two policemen in Austin, Texas, stopped Leno McGarity on a traffic violation. McGarity was accompanied by his three-year-old son. While one officer was writing a ticket, the three-year-old held up his father's .38 revolver and told the second officer, "My daddy has one just like yours, and he keeps his dope right here."

McGarity was booked for unlawfully carrying a weapon and possession of marijuana.
Miami Herald

TRUE matrimony

An English court granted a divorce to Doris and Albert May, who been married for twenty-six years, after Doris charged that Albert ran around naked playing the tambourine outside their house whenever she rejected his sexual advances, and Albert charged that Doris made him pay £4 each time that they slept together.

Irreconcilable differences, ruled the judge.

Memphis Commercial Appeal

TRUE business

A large force of police was called to restrain frenzied mobs in Rio de Janeiro as they attempted to lynch two men who had been charged with the voodoo murder of a two-year-old boy.

The child was allegedly sacrificed to ensure the success of a new cement business.

New York Post

TRUE crime

Ronald Marks was arrested and brought to trial for shoplifting in Ilford, England, found innocent, and released. New charges were filed, however, after police discovered Marks had left the courtroom with a juror's coat.
Eugene Register-Guard

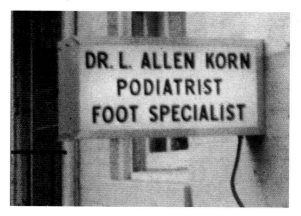

TRUE government

State Representative Jim Kaster has filed a bill in the Texas Legislature that would require criminals to give their intended victims twenty-four hours notice before committing a crime against them.

The bill permits notification either orally or in writing and specifies that the victims be notified of their right to use deadly force to resist.

"I'm not optimistic about the bill's passage with all the lawyers we've got around here," admitted Kaster.

Atlanta Journal and Constitution

LIVES OF THE GREAT

GENERAL DOUGLAS MacARTHUR
(1880-1964)

MEMORABLE QUOTE: "IN WAR, A NATION WHICH DOES NOT WIN, MUST FACE THE CONSEQUENCES OF DEFEAT."

IN THE PHILIPPINES, MACARTHUR USED AN ARMY JEEP WHILE TRAVELING WITH HIS TROOPS, BUT WHEN ALONE PREFERRED A PACKARD LIMOUSINE WHICH HE KEPT STOWED IN THE JUNGLE.

MACARTHUR WAS PLAGUED BY ATTACKS OF NAUSEA DURING MOMENTS OF TENSION. ONCE, FOLLOWING A HEATED DEBATE WITH FDR, HE VOMITED AT THE PRESIDENT'S FEET ON THE STEPS OF THE WHITE HOUSE.

ON JANUARY 26, 1942, MACARTHUR CELEBRATED HIS BIRTHDAY WITH A SURPRISE ATTACK ON THE JAPANESE— TO BOOST THE MORALE OF HIS TIRED TROOPS, HE CLAIMED.

WHEN MACARTHUR ARRIVED AT WEST POINT IN 1899, HE WAS ACCOMPANIED BY HIS SOMEWHAT OVERBEARING MOTHER, WHO REMAINED NEARBY UNTIL 1901, MAKING THE YOUNG CADET THE A TARGET OF MUCH HAZING.

TRUE androgyny

TRUE fact

How to say "bowwow" in eleven languages.

Chinese .... wungwung
Czech .... hafhaf
Dutch .... wafwaf
Finnish .... hauhau
French .... woawoa
German .... wauwau
Hebrew .... havhav
Icelandic.......... voffvoff
Portuguese ...... auau
Russian .... gavgav
Spanish .... jaujau

TRUE hooking

Chief Luis Torres of the San Juan, Puerto Rico, police has ordered his vice-squad agents to stop having sexual intercourse with prostitutes to secure convictions against them.
San Francisco Chronicle

TRUE catch

Aniceto Villarta, thirty-five, was fishing off of Cebu, one of the Philippine Islands, when he brought in a fish and clasped it between his teeth to remove the hook.

But the fish was still alive, and it wiggled into his throat. Despite the efforts of his friends to dislodge the fish, Villarta was suffocated. *UPI*

TRUE medicine

A forty-two-year-old man from Ponce, Puerto Rico, came to the local hospital complaining of a pain in his shoulder. When doctors examined him, they discovered two inches of coat-hanger wire protruding from his rectum.

An X ray disclosed that he had a soft-drink bottle protruding into the peritoneal cavity of his lower abdomen. The man eventually admitted that he had attempted to give himself an enema with a carbonated beverage and that the bottle somehow became lodged in his rectal area. When he couldn't get it out, he fashioned a hook from a coat hanger and had his wife fish with it for the bottle. An operation to remove the accumulated flotsam was successful.

Journal of the American Medical Association

TRUE family

A mother and her two sons shot and wounded each other during a fight over which television program to watch.

"I had just done scrubbing and wanted to watch a quiz show," Mrs. Clara Barton of Dixon, Illinois, told police after the incident.

Mrs. Barton became angry when her son Joey, fourteen, kept changing channels, and slapped him. At that point, her other son, Rick, sixteen, joined the argument, and she picked up a .22 caliber pistol loaded with bird shot and shot the older boy in the legs. A scuffle then ensued in the course of which all three suffered multiple wounds.

"It was an unfortunate situation," said Sgt. William Killiam of the Dixon police. *Chicago Daily News*

TRUE revenge

Michael Hight was accused of mailing an explosive device to a friend of his ex-wife. Hight reportedly blamed Bonnie Winger for the breakup of his marriage, and sent her a phony valentine along with a dildo stuffed with explosive black powder.

Indianapolis Star

GENTLEMEN PLAYERS ARE REQUESTED TO ONLY WASH THEIR BALLS IN THE SINKS PROVIDED AND NOT ELSEWHERE.
J THOMAS Honorary Secretary Newport Golf and Country Club
30 TH JUNE   1862

TRUE fact

Jane Fonda, who, on a visit to Hanoi made antiwar broadcasts over North Vietnamese radio, was Miss Army Recruiting in 1962.

National Review

TRUE error

One morning in May, an insurance salesman on his way to work on Wall Street was standing near the open doors of a New York subway car that had stopped at a station, when a short, well-dressed man entered the car, bumped into him, then abruptly left again. The insurance salesman instinctively felt for his wallet and, finding it missing, reached out and grabbed the short man by his jacket collar.

The subway doors closed with their rubber edges around the salesman's wrists, but he held on even after the car started moving, and managed to drag the other man several feet along the station platform before the material of the man's jacket tore, leaving him holding a few inches of tweed in his hands.

Ten minutes after the insurance salesman reached his office, still fuming at the incident, his wife called to tell him that he had left his wallet at home.

New York Times

TRUE bullshit

A man fell into a pit full of cow dung near Ahmedabad, India. Fortunately, he was in one of the few places on earth where six passersby were willing to dive in after him. Unfortunately, they all died.

Reuters

TRUE bulls

TRUE wildlife

In Madison, Minnesota, an eight-point buck deer attacked a four-hundred-pound cement deer in front of a farmhouse. The horns of the real deer became entangled with those of the lifesize, decorative deer, which then fell off its pedestal. The cement deer broke the real deer's neck in the fall. *Seattle Times*

TRUE homelife

Sipche, a village in northern Nepal not far from Katmandu, has no men in it. According to a recent official census, the women of the village for some reason believed that the one-hundredth man they killed would turn into gold and make them rich, and at the same time help them get into heaven.

The women apparently lured the men to a feast, at which they were fed dishes mixed with harital, a poisonous root. The village is now entirely inhabited by children and widows.

London Express

• LIVES OF THE GREAT •

THOMAS ALVA EDISON (1847–1931)

MEMORABLE QUOTE: A SUCCESSFUL INVENTION IS "SOMETHING SO PRACTICAL THAT A POLISH JEW WILL BUY IT."

EDISON ASKED HIS SECOND WIFE TO MARRY HIM IN MORSE CODE, AND NICKNAMED HIS FIRST TWO CHILDREN "DOT" AND "DASH."

EDISON, THE INVENTOR OF THE PHONOGRAPH WAS NEARLY DEAF (THE RESULT OF HIS BEING PICKED UP BY THE EARS AS A CHILD). HE DID, HOWEVER, ENJOY LISTENING TO RECORDED MUSIC, AS LONG AS IT WAS CLASSICAL AND PLAYED BACKWARDS.

A TIRELESS WORKER WHO OFTEN PREFERRED TO SLEEP STANDING UP, EDISON ONCE INVENTED A HELICOPTER THAT WAS FUELED BY OLD TICKER TAPE. UPON COMPLETING A PROJECT, HE WOULD "SWEAR SOMETHING AWFUL" AND "JUMP UP AND DOWN AND DO A KIND OF ZULU WAR DANCE."

LOOKING OUT FROM HIS HOUSE AT THE NEW JERSEY COUNTRYSIDE, EDISON ONCE SAID, "I'M LOOKING TO MAKE IT MORE BEAUTIFUL. I'M GOING TO DOT IT WITH FACTORIES."

TRUE surrealism

TRUE salesmanship

A door-to-door magazine salesman had his solicitation permit revoked this week following numerous complaints concerning his sales methods.

According to police, the offender, an employee of Opportunity Services Co., Inc., of Michigan City, Indiana, had called upon a woman in the hopes of selling her a magazine subscription. When she failed to express sufficient interest, the salesman unzipped his trousers and urinated in her hallway.
The Iowa City Press Citizen

TRUE crime

Blaine Gregory Gould, twenty-two, of St. John, New Brunswick, was fined $250 after pleading guilty to the charge of misleading a police officer.

The prosecution revealed that Gould had deep-fried his pet gerbil and then pretended to find it in a box of fried chicken purchased at a local takeout restaurant.

Kitchener Waterloo Record

TRUE judgement

When police in Normal, Illinois, arrested twenty-one-year-old Brad Frericks for driving under the influence of alcohol, his roommate, Tim Hall, came to pick him up. But police drove Frericks home themselves after deciding that Hall was also drunk. Later, police arrested Hall as he drove home, then re-arrested Frericks when he came to bail out Hall.

Bloomington Normal Pantagraph

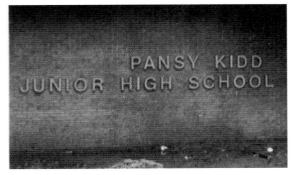

TRUE verdict

Twenty-seven-year-old Carmon Leo complained that a rear-end auto collision turned him into a homosexual.

Although his only physical injury was to his back, Leo said the accident had a jarring effect on his personality and altered his sexuality. The back injury kept him from work for six months, robbing him of his masculinity, Leo said.

"When I found I couldn't function in the business world and support my wife, the effect was emasculating."

According to his attorney, after the accident, Leo left his wife, moved in with his parents and started hanging around gay bars and reading homosexual literature.

The Wayne County Circuit Court Jury awarded him $200,000. The jury also awarded his wife $25,000.

Akron Beacon Journal

TRUE editorial

"It's bad enough that Columbus has so many prostitutes . . . but—pound for pound—we must have some of the heaviest and homeliest hookers in the country."

Columbus, Ohio, Citizen-Journal

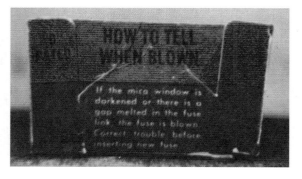

TRUE diet

When jailers checked Eduardo Nedilskyj's cell in Maywood, California, they discovered he had chewed off four of his own fingers to the first knuckle. As doctors attempted to sew the digits back on, Nedilskyj's wife was recovering in another hospital from the attack that resulted in his arrest.

He had bitten off her nose.

UPI

TRUE kink

S&M LOCK & KEY SERVICE
WESTFIELD, N.Y.
PH. 326-3614

S&M COMMUNION BREAD

GRANDMA GRUNT'S GIFT SHOP
HANDMADE LEATHER GOODS

S&M Toy Outlet & Gifts
REAR ENTRANCE
TOYS • FABRICS
GIFTS • CARDS

S&M Restaurant
PRIME RIB
STEAK & LOBSTER
RAINBO TROUT RIBS
FAMILY BUFFET

S·M CLUTCH BRAKE CO.

S & M Clutch & Brake Co.

S&M Restaurant

TRUE rehabilitation

Officials at the Santa Clara county jail in California have released statistics showing that the number of fights among inmates there has declined by one-third since a holding cell was painted pink.
UPI

TRUE daring-do

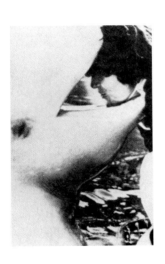

•LIVES OF THE GREAT•

CHARLES SPENCER CHAPLIN (1889-1977)

CHARLIE, WHO PLAYED ONE OF THE WORLD'S MOST LOVED FILM CHARACTERS, WAS CHARACTERIZED IN A PATERNITY SUIT AGAINST HIM AS "A LITTLE RUNT OF A SVENGALI, MASTER MECHANIC OF SEDUCTION, AND A CHEAP COCKNEY CAD."

THE "LITTLE TRAMP" HAD A SERIOUS PENCHANT FOR YOUNG GIRLS. HE MARRIED A SIXTEEN-YEAR-OLD WHEN HE WAS TWENTY-NINE, A FIFTEEN-YEAR-OLD AT THIRTY-FIVE, AND A SEVENTEEN-YEAR-OLD AT FIFTY-FOUR.

ASHAMED OF HIS URCHIN CHILDHOOD, CHAPLIN BECAME FURIOUS WHEN HIS BROTHER REVEALED THAT THE TWO OF THEM OFTEN FED FROM LONDON GARBAGE CANS. AMONG OTHER THINGS THAT BOTHERED HIM WERE TELEPHONES AND OPEN WINDOWS.

IN 1942, AN IRATE GIRL FRIEND HELD CHAPLIN AT GUNPOINT FOR AN HOUR AND A HALF UNTIL HE MADE LOVE TO HER. TWO YEARS LATER, SHE BROUGHT A PATERNITY SUIT AND WON.

ALTHOUGH ALL EVIDENCE INDICATES THE CONTRARY, CHAPLIN REPEATEDLY INSISTED HE WAS JEWISH.

TRUE marketing

TRUE termination

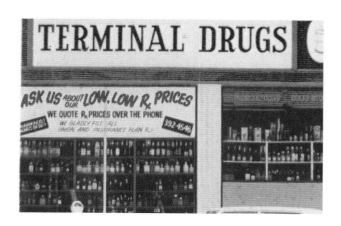

TRUE crime

TRUE suspect

TRUE sport

TRUE irony

Police arrested forty-six-year-old Edward Morris and charged him with sexually assaulting a thirteen-year-old male at the Let's Play Games store in Rockville, Maryland.
The Montgomery County Journal

TRUE military

From an article by Col. John W. Oswalt (Ret.) that discussed the development of vertical takeoff and landing aircraft:

Referring to the midair switch from vertical to horizontal flight, Colonel Oswalt wrote: "The safety people were concerned that should there be a power failure during this transition, the aircraft would certainly crash. To keep the pilot from being apprehensive about this situation, the engineers designed a new instrument for the instrument panel. From the front it merely looked like a black hole. However, behind the panel was mounted a .38 caliber revolver, which, when the engine failed, would shoot the pilot in the head, thus removing all apprehension.
Aviation Digest

TRUE military 2

Canadian troops stationed in Germany were issued the following directive:

Canadian soldiers are now forbidden to faint in an unseemly way while on parade. To avoid the possibility of fainting, a soldier should make sure he has had breakfast on the morning of parade day. If worse comes to worse and he must faint, a soldier should fall to the ground under control. To do so, he must turn his body approximately 45 degrees, squat down, roll to the left and retain control of his weapon to prevent personal injury and minimize damage to his weapon.
Washington Star

REAR ENTRANCE ANAS BUILDING

Welcome to this sign

LOONEY HOUSE →

TRUE crime

Twenty-two-year-old Michael Brez, bearing tattoos of swastikas and the words "White Death" was charged with driving while intoxicated, after he crashed into the back of a truck at thirty miles per hour in Lakeland, Florida.

Accompanied by two teenage girls and an ice-cream cooler full of beer, Brez had been driving a Pinky Dinky Ice Cream truck.

The Lakeland Ledger

Welcome to... WOODVILLE
LIME CENTER OF THE WORLD
SPONSORED BY LOCAL BUSINESS

Hungry Mother State Park NEXT EXIT

TRUE sensitivity

School administrators in Omaha, Nebraska, were discussing a ban on racial epithets such as "nigger" and "honky" when a black member of the board objected. Lawrence McVoy claimed that "nigger" should be banned but "honky" should not, since it was a "complimentary term" that referred to white people's "reputed ancestry from the Huns." David Wilken, a white board member, objected. "I don't buy it," he said.

"Some honkies buy it and some honkies don't." McVoy replied.

UPI

TRUE jumpers

·LIVES OF THE GREAT·

WINSTON CHURCHILL (1874-1965)

"I HAVE SELDOM MET ANYBODY WITH STRANGER GAPS OF
KNOWLEDGE, OR WHOSE MIND WORKED IN GREATER JERKS."
--LORD HALIFAX

AT SIXTEEN, WINSTON
WROTE TO HIS MOTHER
FROM SCHOOL:
"PLEASE DO DO DO DO
DO DO COME DOWN
TO SEE ME." AT
TWENTY-FOUR
HE WROTE HIS
MOTHER FROM
EGYPT: "AVAIL
YOURSELF OF THE
CONSOLATIONS
OF PHILOSOPHY AND
REFLECT ON THE UTTER
INSIGNIFICANCE OF ALL
HUMAN BEINGS."

AS A YOUNG ARMY OFFICER
IN INDIA, WINSTON HAD
A BUNGALOW, A BUTLER,
TWO DRESSING BOYS,
A GROOM FOR EACH
OF HIS POLO
PONIES, TWO
GARDENERS,
THREE WATER
CARRIERS,
FOUR WASHER-
MEN, AND A
WATCHMAN. HE
FOUND LIFE THERE
"STUPID, DULL, AND
UNINTERESTING."

CHURCHILL
WAS KNOWN
TO CARRY
WORMS AWAY
FROM GOLF
COURSES SO
THEY WOULD
NOT BE
TRAMPLED.

STOP--
WORMS

VISITING
FRONT LINE
TRENCHES IN
WWI, CHURCHILL
DECLARED, "I DO NOT
KNOW WHEN I HAVE PASSED A MORE
JOYOUS THREE WEEKS... IT'S A JOLLY LIFE."

TRUE duh!

TRUE shrubbery

A resident of Deloraine, Tasmania, complained to police that a tree growing on his neighbor's property had been trimmed into the shape of an emu, complete with eyes that looked directly into a window of his home.

Police referred the matter to the town council.

Tasmanian Advocate

TRUE

TRUE birding

Abdel Brim Talal was arrested by police in Syros, Greece, after he sodomized a male pelican. Police had to rescue the twenty-eight-year-old Moroccan from an angry mob of locals who had regarded the pelican as a mascot. The pelican, named Marcos, was found wounded in a public toilet. He died later of internal injuries, and his body was stuffed and given to the townspeople.
The Guardian

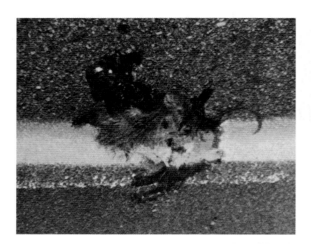

CORRECTION

In the story Saturday about animal control work in Paso Robles, the featured quotation was incorrectly attributed to Robert Dollahite, director of the county Animal Regulation Department.

That statement, "I drive to work everyday watching dead cats getting flatter and flatter" was actually made by Richard Deming, Paso Robles city manager.

San Luis Obispo County
Telegram–Tribune

TRUE death

According to a $3 million wrongful-death suit filed against Disney World in Orlando, Florida, Hattie Richardson had been trying to find her car when she fell into a drainage canal and drowned between the "Minnie" and "Goofy" sections of the Disney World parking lot.

Florida Times Union

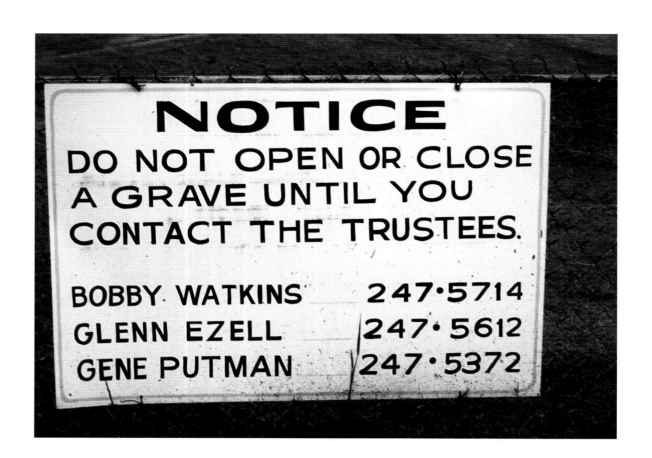

TRUE mortality

TRUE name

Police in North Pownal, New York, arrested a Hoosick Falls man in connection with the theft of a vehicle in which he was found sleeping. The man's name was Ralph Wideawake.
AP

For Honey
Honk Horn

STAY·AWAY
DO NOT TOUCH FENCES
DO NOT TOUCH ANIMALS
NO FOOD — NO WOOD
NO GAS — NO PHONE
NO WATER — NO TOOLS
NOTHING
FOR·SALE
DO·NOT·ENTER

SNACK SHOP
nookie's
BREAKFAST

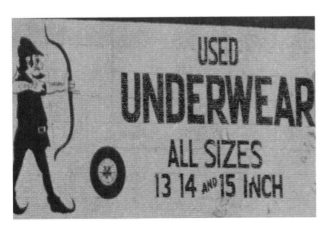

USED
UNDERWEAR
ALL SIZES
13 14 AND 15 INCH

TRUE nitpicking

According to a proposed "Bill of Vengeance" considered by Iranian lawmakers, a person who criminally injures someone will have the same wound inflicted on him as punishment. To guarantee accuracy in such cases, the bill would require that the victim's wounds be measured for length, width, and depth, except for skull wounds, which would not have to be measured for depth.
Boston Globe

TRUE houses

CORRECTION

Current regrets describing the offices of NPR Ventures as "plush" in the March 25 issue. Although there is a couch in the reception area that could be described as plush, on closer inspection the offices proved to be just ordinary.

A Nov. 9 Southam News story about Nova Scotia's black minority was accompanied by an inaccurate photograph caption. The photo, said to depict rundown homes outside Dartmouth, was actually of a pig farm. *The Citizen* apologises for the error.

Father Gene Fabre, a Catholic priest who ran a home for mentally handicapped children in Montpellier, France, was sentenced to ten years in prison for hanging a thirteen-year-old epileptic to death in a straightjacket. Fabre testified that the child was being punished for "disrupting a Sunday Mass with incoherent noises." He also admitted to other disciplinary abuses, such as stuffing girls' mouths with bird droppings and immersing their heads in toilets.

"These aren't really methods." Fabre stated, "but rather tricks that I invented. The conditioning of the handicapped by violence is necessary to compel them to acquire a sense of responsibility."

The priest went on to assure the court that his tricks "worked."
UPI

LIVES OF THE GREAT

MAYOR FRANK RIZZO
OF PHILADELPHIA (1920-1991)

THE FORMER POLICE CHIEF OF PHILADELPHIA IS ALMOST CERTAINLY THE ONLY AMERICAN TO REMAIN IN OFFICE AFTER FAILING A LIE DETECTOR TEST.

WHEN PHILADELPHIA DEMOCRATIC CHAIRMAN P.J. CAMIEL PUBLICLY ACCUSED RIZZO OF OFFERING HIM THE CHANCE TO CHOOSE CONTRACTORS FOR LUCRATIVE CITY PROJECTS IN EXCHANGE FOR ALLOWING RIZZO TO CHOOSE THE CANDIDATE FOR DISTRICT ATTORNEY, THE MAYOR DENIED THE CHARGES AND OFFERED TO TAKE A LIE DETECTOR TEST.

THE TEST INDICATED SIX OUT OF TEN ANSWERS WERE DISHONEST.

WHEN THE MAYOR CROSSED PARTY LINES TO SUPPORT THE REPUBLICAN CANDIDATES IN THE SAME ELECTIONS HE HAD BEEN ACCUSED OF TRYING TO TAMPER WITH, THE RESULTING REPUBLICAN TURNOUT WAS ONE OF THE LOWEST IN PHILADELPHIA'S HISTORY.

SOON AFTER RIZZO MOVED INTO A $77,000 HOME, A REASSESSMENT DROVE THE VALUE OF THE HOUSE UP TO A SURPRISING $155,000. WHEN THE MAYOR TURNED HIS ATTENTIONS TO HIS CITY HALL OFFICE, SPENDING $130,000 OF TAXPAYERS' MONEY IN RENOVATIONS, A GRAND JURY WAS CONVENED TO INVESTIGATE THE SITUATION.

IN MAY, 1973, RIZZO WAS ACCUSED OF TAPPING THE PHONES OF TWO EX-MAYORS OF PHILADELPHIA. IN ADDITION, IT WAS LATER ESTABLISHED THAT RIZZO USED A SPECIAL SQUAD OF CITY POLICEMEN TO KEEP TABS ON HIS POLITICAL ENEMIES.

TRUE existentialism

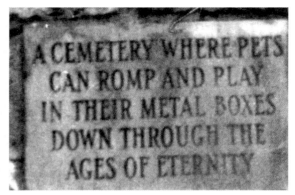

A four-year-old boy from Seymour, Missouri, died during a Memorial Day visit to the grave of his grandfather.

The tombstone fell on his head.
UPI

On the Danish island of Fyn, an oven wall was blown out and a worker suffered shock when the pacemaker in a dead woman's body exploded during cremation. *UPI*

TRUE lodging

Daryl Tichenor, publisher of a weekly, newspaper in Virginia City, Montana, offered a public apology .after his paper, the *Madisonian*, published an article called "blatantly racist" by Anne MacIntyre, administrator of the Montana Human Rights Division.

According to the *Montana Standard* of Butte, the *Madisonian* published a special hunting edition which included a bogus employment application form for minorities.

The application said it wasn't necessary for black applicants to attach a photo, 'since you all look alike.' Mexican applicants were asked to list the time and date they illegally entered the U.S.

If living in an automobile, applicants were instructed to give make, license number, and where parked in lieu of an address.

It asked how many children were claimed for welfare purposes and how many, if any, were legitimate. And it asked income from three sources: thefts, welfare, and unemployment.

Blacks were asked to check off employment experience from these choices: government employee, tap dancer, demonstration leader, singer, evangelist, dope pusher, V. D. spreader, all of these.

Mexicans faced this list: lettuce picker, nose picker, orange picker, lemon picker, tomato picker, city employee, governor of Arizona.

One question said, Check any machines you can operate by yourself: typewriter, TV, adding machine, Coke machine, wheelbarrow, washing machine, slot machine.

Applicants also were asked to list their greatest desire in life other than a white woman in fifty words or less, if they knew that many.

In a front-page editorial following the furor, Tichenor said, "If I did offend any of these minority folks, I sincerely apologize, as that was not the intent."

TRUE intent

TRUE minstrels

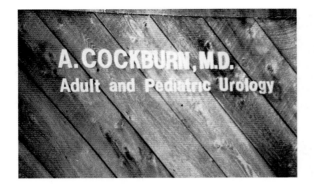

TRUE help

Left to guard his employer's house and pet monkey, John Mwambe of Lusaka, Zambia, killed then roasted the monkey. He fell asleep after dining on the pet, and thieves broke into the house. "The monkey bit me, so I ate it," he later told authorities.

"I didn't hear the thieves."

Ottawa Journal

TRUE economics

A restaurant in the Chinese city of Jilin ran out of dog meat, so the owner put up a notice offering to buy dogs from local citizens. "In less than one month, 1,369 dogs were bought," according to the Chinese Communist party newspaper People's Daily, "a supply that can last one year for this restaurant." The newspaper commended the owner for using capitalist-style enterprise in buying dogs directly from the people instead of "waiting for some central government organization to ship him dog meat."

UPI

TRUE planets

TRUE parenting

A young city-dwelling mother brought her tiny daughter on an outing to a Canadian national park. They soon encountered a large bear, whereupon the woman attempted to stage a cute photographic pose: daughter feeding honey to a bear.

She poured a jar of honey on the infant's hands, positioned her beside the bear, and focused the camera just in time to see the bear eat the little girl's hands.

"Their whole idea of nature and animals has come from Walt Disney," the park director stated.
CP

TRUE houses

·LIVES OF THE GREAT·

TYRUS RAYMOND "TY" COBB
"THE GEORGIA PEACH" (1886-1961)

THE HALL-OF-FAMER'S GAME BEHAVIOR WAS LEGEND. HE ONCE RUSHED INTO THE STANDS AND BEAT A PARAPLEGIC FAN SENSELESS FOR HECKLING HIM. COBB AVENGED BEANBALLING PITCHERS BY BUNTING TO FIRST, WHICH FORCED THEM TO COVER THE BAG, AND THEN SPIKING THEM.

COBB, WHO ONCE BEAT UP A LITTLE FAT KID WHEN HE MISSED A WORD IN A SPELLING BEE, WAS SO DISLIKED BY FANS THAT HE RECEIVED THIRTEEN DEATH THREATS ON ONE ROAD TRIP. WHEN ACCOSTED BY THREE MEN IN DETROIT, HE BEAT TWO OF THEM TO DEATH AND SPAT ON THEIR BODIES.

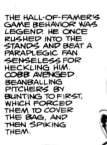

COBB IS BELIEVED TO HAVE ACQUIRED HIS VIOLENT DISPOSITION SHORTLY AFTER HIS MOTHER BLEW HIS FATHER'S HEAD OFF WITH A SHOTGUN.

AS AN OLD MAN, COBB DRANK A QUART OF WHISKEY A DAY AND CARRIED A LUGER EVERYWHERE HE WENT, AS WELL AS AN OLD PAPER BAG CONTAINING OVER ONE MILLION DOLLARS IN NEGOTIABLE SECURITIES.

TRUE navigation

TRUE consistency

TRUE sensitivity

Spurred by a Department of Health, Education, and Welfare investigation, the town of Pekin, Illinois, has changed the name of its various athletic teams from the Chinks to the Dragons. *UPI*

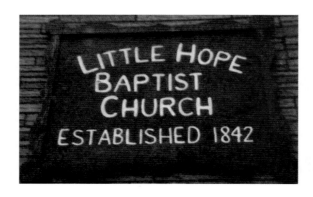

TRUE concessions

Police in Norfolk, Virginia, arrested Kenneth Harsh and charged him with disorderly conduct after he refused to surrender a bag containing a cookie to a theater usher who had instructed Harsh that food from sources other than the theater snack bar was prohibited. Harsh contended that he satisfied his obligation to the theater by purchasing a box of popcorn at an earlier time and, as he testified at his trial, that the charge was unfounded because he didn't intend to eat the cookie until after the show. Harsh produced the cookie and sack in court to corroborate his story and was acquitted.

Chicago Tribune

TRUE theodores

TRUE fat

A 350-pound man named Richard Avella entered a jewelry store on Long Island, pointed a gun at the clerk, announced a holdup, then tripped and fell to the floor. He was unable to get up before police arrived.

New York Daily News

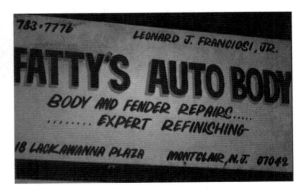

TRUE royalty

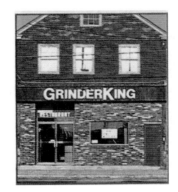

more TRUE royalty

An eighteen-year-old man was arrested after allegedly stealing $6.50 worth of Yumbos from a Burger King in Columbus, Ohio. His name is Ronald McDonald.

The Columbus Dispatch

TRUE zoology

Vernon Wicomb was picnicking with his wife and two children in the Platteklip Gorge near Cape Town, South Africa, when a gang of baboons grabbed their supplies. Wicomb scrambled up a tree and his family ran off screaming while six baboons scooped up a bottle of wine, cigarettes, and a six-pack of beer, then fled to the bush, stashed the liquor and cigarettes, returned to the picnic site, and stole Wicomb's wallet and car keys.

"The animals were very aggressive," Wicomb said. *UPI*

TRUE heimlich

TRUE numbering

A thirty-three-year-old German-American, Michael Dengler, petitioned the state of Minnesota to change his legal name to 1069, claiming the number "symbolizes [his] interrelationship with society and conceptually reflects [his] personal and philosophical identity." When Dengler's petition was refused, he appealed to the Minnesota Supreme Court, which upheld the decision and advised Dengler that under Minnesota law Ten Sixty-nine or One Zero Six Nine would be more acceptable. Judges allowed, however, that anyone wishing to call Dengler 1069 informally may continue to do so.

Newsday

LIVES OF THE GREAT
ALBERT EINSTEIN, 1879-1955

WHILE ALBERT EINSTEIN WAS RESIDING IN PRINCETON, THE ELDERLY SCIENTIST WOULD OFTEN FORGET WHERE HE LIVED. ONCE, STOPPING A PEDESTRIAN ON THE STREET, EINSTEIN EXCLAIMED, "HELLO, I'M ALBERT EINSTEIN. COULD YOU TELL ME WHERE I LIVE?"

WHILE WALKING ABOUT IN ONE OF HIS TYPICAL DAZES, EINSTEIN MANAGED TO WALK DIRECTLY INTO AN OPEN MANHOLE. A PHOTOG- RAPHER WHO CAPTURED THIS EVENT WAS BRIBED INTO SUPPRESSING THE PICTURE.

AS A YOUTH, EINSTEIN WAS SO INEPT AT ACADEMICS AND SPORTS THAT HIS FATHER BELIEVED HIM TO BE RETARDED. EVEN AS AN ADULT, EINSTEIN COULD NOT MASTER THE COM- PLEX TASK OF DRIVING A CAR.

EINSTEIN MARRIED HIS ONCE-DIVORCED COUSIN, ELSA EINSTEIN. IN A STATEMENT ABOUT HIS DEEP LOVE FOR HER, EINSTEIN SAID, "MRS. EINSTEIN IS AN EXCELLENT COOK. IF SHE WEREN'T, I WOULD DIVORCE HER."

IN A 1944 LETTER TO TRUMAN, EINSTEIN SUGGESTED THE CREATION OF AN AMERICAN-RUSSIAN STATE WHICH WOULD CONTROL THE WORLD.

WHEN QUESTIONED ON THE NEGATIVE ASPECTS OF NUCLEAR POWER, EINSTEIN PROCLAIMED, "NUCLEAR POWER IS NO MORE UNNATURAL THAN SAILING A BOAT."

TRUE wager

TRUE love

Love-Organ

SHERWOOD – Mary Theresa Organ and Robert Sterling Love were married Saturday in Immaculate Conception Catholic Church by the Rev. John O'Donnell. Parents are Mr. and Mrs. Thomas P. Organ and Mr. and Mrs. Robert E. Love, all of Sherwood.

Honor attendants were Lori Howard and Victor Cummings.

The couple will reside in North Little Rock.

Cox-Held

Married June 10 at St. Joseph's Catholic Church were Angie M. Cox, Marion, and Rick H. Held, Orlando, Fla. The Rev. John McDermott performed the 2 p.m. ceremony. A reception for 200 guests followed at Longbranch Supper Club.

MRS. MUSTARD
. . . Allison Pickels

Mustard-Pickels

Allison Leilani Pickels and Charles Stoll Mustard Jr., both of Athens, Ga., were married March 24.

Roberts-Pinkstaff

Cheryl F. Pinkstaff and Arthur L. Roberts Jr. were married March 9 at Los Altos Methodist Church.

The bride is the daughter of Robert A. Akins Sr., Louisville, Ky., and Sadie M. Moles, Hurricane, W.Va. A graduate of Milpitas High School and San Jose State University, she is a police officer in Newark.

The bridegroom is the son of Arthur L. Roberts Sr. and Ruth A. Roberts, Mountain View.

Kuntz-Dick

Lisa Renee Kuntz and Gary Wayne Dick plan to be married in a 12:30 p.m. ceremony July 14 at Carmel United Methodist Church in Carmel, Ind.

BUNN-GRABS

KING — Ashley Elizabeth Grabs of King and Kevin Brett Bunn of Raleigh were married Saturday at King Moravian Church.

The bride is the daughter of Mr. and Mrs. Omnie Omily Grabs Jr. of King. Parents of the bridegroom are Mr. and Mrs. Franklin Bunn of Raleigh.

Bunn

After a reception at King Recreation Acres, the couple left on their wedding trip to Florida. They will live in Raleigh.

Swallows, Cox

DOTHAN, Ala. — Alicia Ann Swallows and Rutledge Eugene Cox Jr. were married at 7 p.m. Dec. 12 at First United Methodist Church.

The Revs. Jerry Dooling and Dr. Carlisle Miller officiated.

The bride is the daughter of Arliene W. Swallows and the late C. Arnold Swallows.

The bridegroom is the son of Mr. and Mrs. Rutledge E. Cox Sr. of Charleston, S.C.

Maid of honor was Emily Roe. Attendants were Sharla Beaty, Sharon Beaty, Julie Jones, Barbara Kamensky, Sally Lester and Beth Martinez.

The father of the bridegroom was best man. Ushers were Shaun Ballard, Rick Brandon, Randy Cox, Raymond Cox, Art Deas and Bob Dollar.

A reception was held at the church.

The bride graduated from Auburn University. She is a pharmacist for Super-D in Memphis, Tenn.

The bridegroom graduated from the University of Charleston. He is a district manager for Glaxo Drug in Memphis.

MRS. R.E. COX JR.
. . . Alicia Ann Swallows

Street - Lay

Mr. and Mrs. Dean Street of Toledo are pleased to announce the engagement of their daughter, Diane Lynn, to Lonnie T. Lay, son of Mr. and Mrs. Arzo Lay of Toledo.

A March 27, 1993 wedding is planned.

Cockman-Dickman

Carrie Anne Cockman, formerly of Davenport, and Dr. Donald G. Dickman, Cheyenne, Wyo., were married May 29 at St. John's Church, Creighton University, Omaha, Neb.

Their attendants were Maureen Maley, Maureen Mullin, Julie Stockert, Peggy Dickman, Pam Dickman, Kari Greguska, Troy Peterson, John Sammis, Ben Lass, Chris Cockman and Joe Cockman.

Their parents are Len and Lory Cockman, Newton, Iowa; and Charles and Shirley Dickman, Cheyenne.

Dr. and Mrs. Donald Dickman

Ball-You

Sophia You, daughter of Mr. and Mrs. Yong Su You of Seoul, South Korea, and Maj. Randall N. Ball, son of Mr. and Mrs. Billy C. Ball of St. Albans, were married May 12 at the Yongsan Military Installation in Seoul.

Good-Loser

Mary Ellen Good of Hummelstown, daughter of Mr. and Mrs. Thomas T. Good of Sutton Avenue, Hopwood, became the bride of Stephen T. Loser, son of Mr. and Mrs. Thomas J. Loser of Hershey on July 1 at St. Joan of Arc Church in Hershey.

The Rev. John Hoke officiated at the service.

Given in marriage by her father, the bride wore a full length blush satin brocade gown with ballgown neckline and sleeves, basque waistline and chapel length train. A veil of illusion fell from a satin headpiece of roses and pearls.

MR., MRS. LOSER

Swallows, Wright

Kim Raquel Swallows and Robert Craig Wright exchanged wedding vows in a 2 p.m. ceremony on July 30 at the Eastside Kirtland Air Force Base Chapel.

The bride is the daughter of Kathleen M. Swallows of Honolulu. The groom's parents are Mr. and Mrs. Keith Wright of Northville, Mich.

Gina Swallows and Deidre Montańo, sisters of the bride, were attendants.

Mrs. Wright

Keith Wright, the groom's father, was best man.

The couple spent their honeymoon in Telluride, Colo. and Durango, Colo.

They are making their home in Rio Rancho, where the bride is a homemaker and the groom is a technical sergeant of Life Support serving in the United States Air Force.

Beaver—Trimmer

NEW OXFORD — St. Paul's "The Pines" Lutheran Church was the setting for the Dec. 15 wedding of Janet L. Beaver and Gary R. Trimmer. The Rev. B. Tim Wagner performed the double ring ceremony at 5 p.m.

A resident of 303 N. Bolton St., the bride is the daughter of Charles and Ann Beaver, Northumberland RD1. The bridegroom is the son of Edwin and Romaine Trimmer, 2147 Hunterstown/Hampton Road, New Chester.

Given in marriage by her father, the bride wore a pale pink wedding gown of satin. It was styled with a natural waistline, and the satin bodice featured a shirred center panel of re-embroidered lace with sequins and pearl drops. The long, satin sleeves had a double shoulder puff which extended into a fitted sleeve of English net and satin. The back bodice featured a deep V and a butterfly satin bow at the waistline.

The full satin skirt was edged at the hemline with a scalloped border of re-embroidered lace. The skirt extended into a sweeping cathedral-length train.

Lisa Tomalavage of Dauphin was the matron of honor. Chosen as the bridesmaids were Melissa Frantz and Sandy Kase, both of No.thumberland. Brittany Beaver of Northumberland was the flower girl.

Serving as the best man was Willie Musselman of York Springs. The ushers were Jeff Murren and Charles Becker, both of Hanover. Jason Trimmer of Abbottstown and Dustin Beaver of Northumberland were the ring bearers.

Ruth Dellinger of Gettysburg provided the organ music. The vocalists were Marcia Knorr of Hanover and Ted Schott of East Berlin.

A reception for 175 guests followed in Heidlersburg Firehall. The newlyweds are living at 489 Frazer Road, Aspers.

The bride is a 1980 graduate of Shikellamy High School and a 1987 graduate of Bloomsburg University. She is pursuing a master's degree at

Mr. and Mrs. Gary Trimmer

Western Maryland College and is a teacher for Lincoln Intermediate Unit No. 12.

The bridegroom is a 1983 graduate of New Oxford High School and is a carpenter and crew leader for Barry Bechtel General Contractor Inc.

Long-Cox

Shannon Marie Cox and Mark Edward Long were married Aug. 30, 1989, at Graceland Wedding Chapel, Las Vegas, Nev.

The bride is the daughter of Dale Cox Jr. of North Aurora and the late Pamela Cox. The groom is the son of Janet Grady of Punta Gorda, Fla., and John Long of Aurora.

The bride is a 1988 graduate of West Aurora High School. She is employed by Farmers Insurance Group. The groom is a 1982 graduate of East Aurora High School. He is employed by Berry Bearing Co.

They live in Aurora.

Mr. and Mrs. Long

TRUE pride

TRUE justice

It is the policy of corrections authorities in Alamos, Mexico, to arrest any prison guard who is on duty when an inmate breaks out, and lock him up for the remainder of the escapee's sentence.
UPI

TRUE justice

A man was sentenced to two months in jail by an Islamic court in Kuala Lumpur, Malaysia, after it received testimony that he had been "moaning with pleasure."

The defendant claimed his moaning was actually occasioned by a high and painful fever, which an alleged woman at his side was "attempting to soothe." However, prosecutor's wit-nesses reiterated that after listening outside the defendants door for fifteen minutes they were absolutely certain the moans arose from pleasure.
Los Angeles Times

TRUE snooker

Arthur Charlton, a window cleaner in London, England, admitted to a divorce court that after his wife left him he moved a snooker table into his bedroom and periodically had a game with a woman friend.

Mrs. Charlton accused her husband of adultery, testifying that on at least one occasion she came home unannounced and heard grunting noises coming from the bedroom.

The grunts were "an expression of surprise after playing a difficult shot," Mr. Charlton explained, but Judge Aubrey Myerson granted Mrs. Charlton the divorce after reasoning that any shot would have been difficult "in a darkened bedroom in the middle of the night."

AP

TRUE vending

Vice detectives arrested forty-one-year-old Dianne Yates at an adult bookstore in Columbus, Ohio, after she was observed performing allegedly obscene acts inside a booth labeled "Fantasy Phone." According to the police report, Yates charged twenty-five cents to act out the sexual fantasies of customers while they described them to her over a telephone.

Police records also indicate that the detectives spent a total of seven quarters before making the arrest.

UPI

TRUE law

Robert Doherty, an attorney in Salem, Virginia, was waiting in his office to meet a client he had agreed to defend on charges of drunk driving when he heard a loud crash. Doherty ran to his reception area, where he found his client sitting in a car he had driven through the front door.
UPI

TRUE monkeyshines

Mrs. On Madrai, a Javanese field-worker in the village of Dawuan, was napping under a tree when an unidentified species of monkey tore off her underwear and raped her. When the woman woke up and realized what was happening, she struggled to disengage herself, then ran screaming into the woods and collapsed from exhaustion. There, the monkey threw her into a bush and raped her once again. Mr. Madrai declined to report the incident to police.

"After all, it was only a monkey," he stated
AFP

TRUE talent

A cockatoo who could roller-skate was among more than three million birds killed in an attempt to halt the spread of an epidemic of Newcastle Disease, a highly contagious malady. The owner of the bird received $2,000 in compensation.

"Before we euthanized him, we had him roller-skate for the last time," explained an appraiser involved in the project.

"Then we gassed him."
Santa Monica Evening Outlook

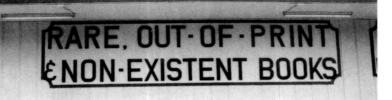

BLIN BOOKM

RARE, OUT-OF-PRINT
& NON-EXISTENT BOOKS

TRUE government

Artist Tom Otterness made a twenty-nine-minute videotape entitled "Shot Dog Film" that was broadcast over a cable channel in New York City. The work, which featured Otterness tying a small dog to a post and shooting it to death, was loudly criticized by the ASPCA and the National Endowment for the Arts, who provided the grant that made the film possible.

New York Daily News

TRUE medicine

A South African boy visited Dr. Solomon Abel, an ophthalmologist in Capetown, after experiencing ten weeks of discomfort in his left eye. After careful examination, Solomon discovered a plant growing in the boy's eyeball. It was tentatively identified as a chrysanthemum.
UPI

LIVES OF THE GREAT

EDMUND G. "JERRY" BROWN
DEMOCRATIC GOVERNOR OF CALIFORNIA

MEMORABLE QUOTE: "THE ONLY WAY A PERSON CAN GET A JOB IN MY CABINET IS IF HE'S A POVERTY LAWYER, A KOOK, OR A PRIEST WHO WORKED WITH CESAR CHAVEZ."

BROWN, WHO ASPIRES TO BE PRESIDENT, HAS CALLED HIS JOB AS GOVERNOR "A PAIN IN THE ASS."

IN A DISCUSSION OF POLICY WITH ADVISERS, BROWN ONCE STATED, "I'LL BELIEVE I HAVE TO DO SOMETHING FOR THE UNEMPLOYED ONLY WHEN THEY START RIOTING IN THE STREET."

BROWN CHOSE TO SUPPORT MEXICANS RATHER THAN BLACKS DURING HIS GUBERNATORIAL CAMPAIGN, SAYING, "BLACKS ARE THE WRONG SYMBOL FOR THE SEVENTIES."

HE LIKES TO SPEND HOURS IN A SLEAZY SACRAMENTO CAFÉ, DRINKING AND DANCING WITH THE MEXICAN WOMEN WHO IDOLIZE HIM.

TRUE logo

A bank robber in Stockton, California, was leaving the Wells Fargo Bank with his loot when he stopped in the lobby to call a taxi.

When police arrived in response to a silent alarm, the robber was sitting quietly in the bank lobby waiting for his cab. *Newscript*

TRUE military

When units of the German army moved into an area north of Munich for maneuvers, a young private was ordered to guard a bridge at the river Amper until relieved. Villagers discovered the soldier three days later crouched under a bus shelter to protect himself from a driving thunderstorm. They gave him food and water, then called the army, whose spokesman admitted that officers had "simply forgotten about him" and moved the troops one hundred miles away.

AP

TRUE medicine

A twenty-year-old hardware-store clerk, Aubrey E. Carter III, was arrested in Miami, Florida, for alleged crimes that earned him the nickname "Dr. Upchuck." According to officials, Aubrey telephoned over 400 female hospital patients last year, identified himself as a doctor, and advised them to "drink two glasses of water, stick [their] finger down their throat, and throw up."

"I think it has some sexual overtones," commented a police sergeant associated with the case.

AP

TRUE government

Residents of Corpus Christi, Texas, voted overwhelmingly in favor of a proposition lowering the city's property-tax ceiling and limiting annual tax increases to 6 percent.

The Corpus Christi City Council retaliated by suing the entire town to recover the money they are now unable to spend.

New York Times

TLUE

TRUE jerk

Lawrence Wright spotted a woman stranded with a flat tire on a Vermont road and stopped to help. He was badly injured, however, when the jack slipped and the weight of her car crushed him between a fender and the pavement. As Wright squirmed in pain, the woman berated him for failing to complete the job, then replaced the lug nuts, jacked the car off his body, told him, "The hospital is just down the road," and drove away.

Wright eventually found his way to an emergency room.

Chicago Tribune

TRUE gripe

James Meredith, the black man who became nationally known in the early sixties as the first student to break the color barrier at the University of Mississippi, was arrested in Jackson on charges of false pretense, a type of larceny where thieves obtain title to property by falsely representing their intent to pay for it.

The property in this case was a pizza owned by Pizza Hut. Meredith allegedly ordered and received two pizzas yet paid for only one of them, on the assumption that a coupon he was holding entitled him to claim the other pizza at no cost.

When the manager pointed out that the coupon actually read "Buy two pizzas and get one free" Meredith became incensed, refused to pay, and was arrested.

New York Times

JAYLYNN STUDIOS

HAVE THE KIDS SHOT FOR DAD FROM $24 95

CAUTION

WALK TIME SHORTENED WHEN TRAIN APPROACHES

LOVELESS BONDING CO.

Disney's Lingerie

TRUE lawman

Rochester, New York, policeman Brian McCoy was reassigned after chief Thomas Hastings ruled that the officer was wrong to shoot a man who was threatening to kill himself with a knife. McCoy appealed the chief's decision, but State Supreme Court Justice John Conway upheld the ruling, supporting the finding that shooting is not an acceptable way to prevent suicide.
UPI

Knox County and the city of Knoxville, Tennessee, were sued for $25,000 by a woman who claimed that a wall-mounted toilet in the City County Building there fell to the floor with her on it. According to the suit, she "now suffers from a fear of toilets...and is forced to search for toilets securely attached to the floor."
Knoxville Journal

TRUE understatement

An unnamed government official flying on a domestic Air Zimbabwe flight opened a curtain in the first-class section where he was seated and urinated on three economy-class passengers. The airline declined comment on the incident, but according to one of the victims on the flight from Garwick to Salisbury, "It was not very nice."
London Daily Telegraph

TRUE services

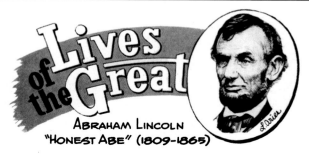

Lives of the Great

ABRAHAM LINCOLN
"HONEST ABE" (1809-1865)

He's a "giraffe," a "creature from Illinois," and an "original gorilla."
— Edwin Stanton

"If anybody wants to kill me, he will do it."
— Lincoln, shortly before he was assassinated.

LINCOLN believed that "physical differences" would prevent blacks from ever becoming equal to whites. In 1863, he approved a plan to relocate thousands of blacks in the Chiriqui coal region of South America (The South Americans rejected it).

WHEN Lincoln's men couldn't find any Indians during the Blackhawk Indian War, they raided farms and distilleries. Superior officers later made Lincoln carry a wooden sword as punishment.

LINCOLN suffered frequent fits of depression and semiconsciousness. Once, while his infant son was being taken for a ride in a wagon, the child fell out. Lincoln continued to pull the empty cart around the neighborhood leaving the baby on the street.

TRUE hubba-hubba

TRUE witness

After Roberto Tercero reported that he had been robbed, police routinely questioned him in hopes of discovering the thief's identity.

When asked if Tercero had noticed anything unusual about the robber's appearance, he replied, "He had popsicle sticks up his nose, gray socks on his hands, and he wore a brown paper bag as a hat."

No arrests have as yet been made.

New York Daily News

TRU mi si g lett rs

TRUE military

In a book on the wartime exploits of the Office of Strategic Services (OSS), R. Harris Smith, a former CIA analyst, revealed that at one time American intelligence officials planned to drive Adolf Hitler insane by exposing him to pornography.

After conducting a long-range psychiatric study that convinced them that the Fuhrer could be unhinged by obscene material, a group of OSS psychoanalysts collected the finest library of German porno ever assembled.

They planned to drop the material by plane over Hitler's' headquarters in Berchtesgaden in the belief that the Nazi dictator would wander outside, see it, and immediately be driven insane.

Unfortunately, the Army Air Corps colonel delegated to organize the smutdrop left his first meeting with the OSS officials in a blind rage, cursing them as maniacs and refusing to jeopardize a single airman's life in the operation.
Winnipeg Tribune

Compliments of:

WEE·WEE
RESTAURANT & DISCO PUB

M.O.A. RICE & PALAY DEALER
62 RIZAL AVE., LUCBAN, QUEZON
TELEPHONE NO. 217

ARCO SWINE & POULTRY FARM
BO. KULAPI, LUCBAN, QUEZON

TRUE irony

Last January, fire totally destroyed the building housing the Capitol Asbestos Fabricators Corporation in Alexandria, Va.

"This is not a fitting end for an asbestos company," said Raymond Layburn, manager of the firm.

New York Post

TRUE crime

Maria Marcon, twenty-four, of Rome, Italy, got off a train and accepted a ride from a dark-haired stranger. Shortly after she entered the car, a three-foot dwarf popped out of a cardboard box on the back seat, clubbed her over the head, and stole $60 from her purse.

When she came to, she was lying on the street.
Canadian Press

TRUE justice

While serving as Los Angeles police chief, Edward M. Davis urged that skyjackers be tried right at the airport and hung on a mobile gallows.

"I would recommend we have a portable courtroom on a big bus and a portable gallows," suggested the police officer, "and after we get the death penalty put back in, we conduct a rapid trial for a hijacker out there, and then we hang him with due process of law out there at the airport."
Los Angeles Times

TRUE verdict

Wan Li, a former employee of the People's Bank of China, was tried for embezzling $52,000 from his office in Peking and sentenced to fifteen years in prison. Charging the term was excessive, Wan appealed his case to the Chinese Supreme Court, which reviewed the case, ruled that the punishment handed down by the lower court was inadequate.

Wan was sentenced to death.
Zodiac News Service

TRUE beauty

Women in Ugley, England, have changed the name of their community service organization from Ugley Women's Institute to the Women's Institute (Ugley Division).
Edmonton Sun

TRUE justice

The California Commission on Judicial Qualifications called for the removal of Los Angeles Municipal Court Judge Leland W. Geiler on the grounds that, among other things, he allegedly prodded a public defender with a dildo.

The commission charged that Judge Geiler invited the public defender into his office and thrust "into the area of the defender's buttocks...a battery-operated object resembling a penis and sometimes referred to as a 'dildo'."

In the courtroom later the same day, the judge reportedly grew weary of the public defender's lengthy cross-examination and twice ordered his clerk "to get the machine out."

"I have no further questions, Your Honor," the defender said, and concluded his argument.
San Francisco Chronicle

Lives of the Great

JULIUS "GROUCHO" MARX
(1890-1977)

"I'm a very bad lay." — After his third marriage.

IN 1928 GROUCHO'S FATHER ATTENDED ONE OF HIS SON'S PERFORMANCES IN NEW YORK, AFTER WHICH GROUCHO RIPPED THE ELDERLY MAN'S SHIRT OFF BECAUSE HE "DIDN'T LIKE" THE SHOW.

GROUCHO, TORMENTED THROUGHOUT HIS LIFE BY PREMATURE EJACULATION, GAVE ONE OF HIS FIANCEES MONEY AFTER EACH DATE AS COMPENSATION.

AT FIFTEEN, GROUCHO CONTRACTED SYPHILIS FROM A PROSTITUTE, THEN SPENT SEVERAL YEARS "SLEEPING WITH COLORED GIRLS." HE AND HIS BROTHERS OFTEN SHARED THE SAME WOMEN — IF ONE BECAME PREGNANT, THEY WOULD SPLIT THE ABORTION COSTS FOUR WAYS.

TRUE desert

TRUE crime

Ling Chao, forty, of Taipei, Taiwan, has been sentenced to death for masterminding the armed robbery of 100,000 eels.

The eels, valued at more than $20,000, were stolen at gunpoint from an eel farm in central Taiwan. *Stars and Stripes*

TRUE customization

TRUE literature

The following excerpts have been culled from unsolicited manuscripts sent to a prominent editor of (serious) fiction who wishes, understandably, to remain anonymous.

The bookcase was made of solid walnuts and polished to a high shine.

The nurse peeped into my bedpan and put it on the floor, whispering "sh."

Her large gray eyes were the window of an unhappy soul which dwelled deep inside her.

His eyes fell instantly on Trudy's black nightgown, which she was occupying.

It seemed like an hour had flown by before he spoke.

Mr. Phillips cleared his throat to make his presents felt.

Murphy let his features slip and he laughed heartily. "Well, you know what they say...all's fair in show business!"

The dishes done, Ruth sat down with a book of cross words.

Francis had hazel eyes and auburn hair with a smooth, creamy complexion—and besides, she had a good head on her shoulders.

Who was she, this wife, this mother of his children, this "Mary" to his "John"?

"Are you terribly well read?" she asked.

He'd always hated being bound and gagged.

Secure in the knowledge that no one could ever spot him as the murderer, Saul acted with all sincerity the part of the grief-stricken friend of the deceased.

He peeled his eyes from the boy's face.

The convict sneered at Bobby as he hugged his pet skunk to his thin chest. "Shut up, squirt," he snarled.

She tried desperately to be fair, weighting the question almost as a butcher would a side of beef on a large set of scales.

If Darcy wanted to invite her to the prom she would be thrilled to say the most.

Being of sound mind and as of yet sound limb, I hereby write this story in the fondest of hopes that someone will read it.

"You've got to find my little boy, officer," she cried, wringing her hands, "I've been keeping his dinner warm for hours!"

The playboy slammed the wardrobe door shut and eyed the girl. "I'd like to know where Kevin fits in all this," he demanded.

The man wore a charcoal-grey three-piece suit and sported a diamond ring on his pinky that Sergeant Miller exaggerated to himself as being the size of a hamburger.

She sank to the floor murmuring, "All for a few lays and some orgasms!" She started to beat her head against the floor. "We'd better go," said her husband. "There's nothing either of us can do here." "One more thing," Dennis suggested. "How about the children?"

Burt didn't wake Lana when he got home and when she woke in the morning his side of the bed wasn't soiled

Her name was Bonnie and she was of female occasion.

Beason's Appliance Store in Lafayette, Indiana, had advertised a "Wizard of Savings" for its customers, but its "Yellow Brick Road Sale" was disrupted when a sudden tornado destroyed the store.
Indianapolis Star

TRUE mortality

TRUE health

TRUE alibi

Berlyn Salazar filed a $250,000 lawsuit against the city of Espanola, New Mexico, after an incident in which, he charged, he was beaten by police. Salazar said that he required emergency surgery after an officer kicked him in the groin.

Commenting on the case, Espanola police chief A. B. Valdez claimed that Salazar, in an effort to implicate the police department, had actually kicked himself in the groin.
Albuquerque Journal

TRUE -onny

According to an obituary for Marjorie Ellen Craw, the fifty-seven-year-old Albany, Indiana, woman left twelve children behind. Their names are Donny, Johnny, Lonny, Vonny, Yonny, Nonny, Onny, Shonny, Connie, Monnie, Bonnie, and Tonnie.
Muncie Evening News

TRUE dames

A two-hundred-pound woman dressed as a tree was arrested for brandishing a knife at a bank teller in Nashville, Tennessee. According to police, the woman wore a sheer dress with cutoff tree limbs tied around her. She was carrying three kitchen knives and rocks in her pockets.
Nashville Banner

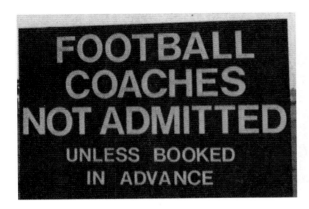

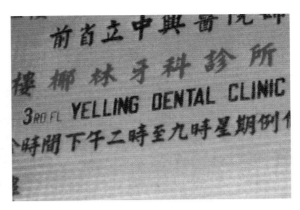

3ʀᴅ ꜰʟ YELLING DENTAL CLINIC

HE'S NOT HERE

NO PARKING THIS SIDE
SUNDAY
MONDAY
TUESDAY
WEDNESDAY
THURSDAY
FRIDAY
SATURDAY

TRUE combat

U.S. soldiers were carrying out war game maneuvers in Darmstadt, Germany, when they spotted what looked like the bivouac of their "aggressor."

They proceeded to attack a Boy Scout encampment.

Larry Groth, scoutmaster of American Troop 21, and his scouts, aged eleven to fifteen, were awakened by M16 rifle fire and floodlights. He finally managed to explain to the forty invading soldiers and their commander that the boys were "friendlies." The commander ordered a cease-fire and apologized. The M16s had been firing blanks.

Groth still can't understand the mistake. The camp had no camouflage, eleven fires burning, civilian cars, and blue and yellow tents. He intends to ask for reimbursement for damage to equipment sustained by the scout camp during the invasion.

The boys, whose behavior was exemplary throughout, are dependents of U.S. Army personnel stationed in the Munich area.

Tampa Tribune Times

TRUE marketing

A family affair. A good time was had by all who attended the Celebrity Rodeo and Longhorn Cattle Drive.

TRUE medicine

A thirty-eight-year-old man showed up at the emergency room of Swedish Hospital in Seattle, Washington, complaining of a burning sensation in his throat. After X-rays revealed a table knife lodged deep in his esophagus, the patient admitted that he had used the knife to dislodge a pill that had become stuck in his throat and had swallowed the blade in the process.

It is not known what became of the pill, an Empirin-3 tablet. *Seattle Post-Intelligencer*

The Thurlows, *pictured here with their daughter Madelaine, were watching* St. Elsewhere *on television when their house in Birmingham, England, caught fire. A fireman said that Mrs. Thurlow and her two daughters continued watching the show as the house burned around them. "One of the daughters was smoking a cigarette. The wife was coughing." Firefighters removed the three women, a dog, and a "big fluffy cat" without injury.*

Baltimore Evening Sun

TRUE progress

Six exotic birds, cockatoos and macaws worth $10,000 were removed from decorative cages in the lobby of the Golden Nugget Casino in Atlantic City New Jersey, because they "were either sleeping or sitting on their perches and weren't lively enough" to suit the casino's managers.

According to casino spokeswoman Muriel Harris, the birds will be replaced by Disneyland-style mechanical birds, which will presumably require less sleep.

"We hope these birds will be a little more animated, fly, and sing softer than the last batch," Harris said.

Philadelphia Inquirer

TRUE snickering (go ahead. it's okay. no one's looking.)

Italian Cheese*
Provolone Balls

1 **44**

½ Lb.
Reg. 3.98 Lb.

• Perfect for Snacks and Cooking
*In our Middletown Gourmet Shop only.

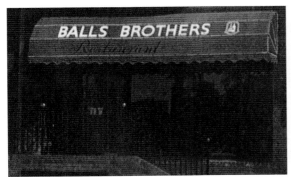

BALLS BROTHERS

Just Balls
SPORTING GOODS

MODERN MENSWEAR

Brass Balls

TIRES

BALL'S WRECKER
24 HOURS SERVICE
PHONE 533-6027
NO JOB TO LARGE OR SMALL

NEW ENGLAND
MINIATURE BALL

L.O. BALLS
WOODSPLITTERS
HYDRAULIC JACK REPAIR

TRUE perversion

TRUE spirtuality

TRUE religion

A delegation from the Yungnara tribe of Australian aborigines has petitioned the United Nations Human Rights Commission to prevent oil drilling around Pea Hill in western Australia. They claim that site is the home of the Great Goanna, their lizard god. If Goanna is disturbed, they say, he will tell the native monitor lizards not to mate, and that could cause a lizard shortage.

Lizards are a major food source for the Yungnaras.
Detroit News

TRUE crime

Police in a motorboat that was out of gas spotted a stolen boat coming through a Rideau Canal lock in Perth, Ontario.

When the two juveniles in the stolen boat saw the sputtering police boat turn their way, they began to jettison heavy items to make a run for it. Among the items they tossed overboard was an auxiliary gas tank.

The policemen fished it from the water, then used the fuel to run down the fleeing craft.
Toronto Sun

TRUE headlines

Man beats off bear
to save his friend

April slated as child abuse month

County wants money for
taking dump

Coke Head To Speak Here

Body search reveals $4,000 in crack

Lebanon will try
bombing suspects

Venereal disease
is linked to crack

Altoona (Pennsylvania) Mirror

Szoka plans drive for priests
to climax during pope's visit

Detroit Free Press

Bloody butt
hurts Ramirez

Chavez still unbeaten in 62 pro fights

Lahaina (Hawaii) News

TRUE crime

Mark Maybry of Albuquerque, New Mexico, was arrested when he attempted to use his mother's Master Charge card in a California liquor store. The card was listed as stolen because she had been found shot to death in her garage, and Mark became implicated when police reportedly found a list in his room which read:

"Things to do:
(1) Buy shells.
(2) Shoot father.
(3) Shoot mother."

Los Angeles Times

more T UE mis ing let ers

TRUE groceries

MAXIMUM ALLOWABLE DEFECTS IN FOOD

Broccoli (frozen):
Average of 60 aphids, thrips, and/or mites per 100 grams.

Chocolate:
Average of 60 microscopic insect fragments per 100 grams; or, average of 1 rodent hair per 100 grams.

Green coffee beans:
Average 10 percent or more by count are insect infested, insect damaged, or moldy; or, 1 live insect in each of 2 containers, or 3 live insects in 1 container.

Potato chips:
6 percent by weight containing rot.

Peanut butter:
Average of 30 insect fragments per 100 grams; or average of 1 or more rodent hairs per 100 grams.

Tomato juice:
Average 10 drosophila fly eggs per 100 grams, or 5 drosophila fly eggs and 1 drosophila maggot per 100 grams, or 2 drosophila maggots per 100 grams.

Tomato paste, pizza; and other sauces:
Average 30 drosophila fly eggs per 100 grams, or 15 drosophila fly eggs and 1 drosophila maggot per 100 grams, or 2 drosophila maggots per 100 grams.

Popcorn:
1 rodent excreta pellet found in 1 or more of 10 225-gram subs, or 6 10-ounce consumer-size packages, provided that 1 or more rodent hairs are found in the other subs; or, 2 rodent hairs per pound with 50 percent of the subs contaminated, or 20 gnawed grains per pound with 50 percent of the subs contaminated with rodent hair, or 5 percent by weight of field corn.

Dried prunes:
Average of 5 percent by count insect infested, moldy, decomposed, dirty, and/or otherwise unfit.

Spinach (canned or frozen):
Average of 50 aphids, thrips, and/or mites per 100 grams; or 2 or more 3-mm larvae and/or larval fragments of spinach worms (caterpillars) whose aggregate length exceeds 12 mm in 24 pounds; or leaf miners of any size, average 8 per 100 grams; or leaf miners 3 mm or longer, average 4 per 100 grams; or average of 10 percent leaves by count or weight; or areas of 1/2 inch diameter affected by mildew or other type of decomposition.

Raisins:
10 whole or equivalent insects and 35 drosophila eggs per 8 ounces of golden bleached raisins.

Strawberries (frozen; whole or sliced):
Average mold count of 45 percent.

Food and Drug Administration

TRUE entertainment

TRUE pets

A New York man, infuriated after one of his family's ten pet cats defecated on the carpet, chased the animal with a loaded sixteen-gauge shotgun. When the cat hid under a chair, the man used the butt of his rifle to prod it into the open for a clear shot.

The cat escaped as the gun discharged into the throat of its master, blowing his brains all over the carpet.

Albany Times Union

TRUE government

When the Department of Commerce discovered that the FCC rulebook contained an incorrect zip code, the commission then issued the following statement:

1. The U.S. Department of Commerce, Environmental Research Laboratories, has notified the commission that the zip code for its facilities at Boulder, Colo., is not correctly printed in sections 73.711, 73.1030 and 74.12 of the commission's rules.

2. The city address zip code in sections 73.711(c)(2), 73.1030(b)(2) and 74.12(c)(2) is corrected to read as follows:

Boulder Colorado 80303

3. We conclude that adoption of the editorial amendment shown in this order will serve the public interest. Prior notice of rule making, effective date provisions and public procedure thereon are unnecessary, pursuant to the administrative procedure and judicial review provisions of 5 U.S.C. 533(b)(3)(B), inasmuch as this amendment imposes no additional burdens and raises no issue upon which comments would serve any useful purpose.

4. Therefore, it is ordered that, pursuant to sections 4(1), 303(r) and 5(a)(1) of the Communications Act of 1934, as amended, and section 0.281 of the commission's rules and regulations, parts 73 and 74 of the commission's rules and regulations, is amended as set forth in paragraph 2 above.

TV Guide

TRUE errors

TRUE bitch

Alpha Xi Delta sorority held a rush party at its house near the University of Texas campus in Austin, Texas.

As eighteen-year-old Regina Gerling waited to enter the party with other rush candidates, she suffered a massive heart attack and dropped dead. Her corpse was removed, and the party continued.

When a sorority member was informed Gerling had died, she replied, "All I know is you're ruining our rush party."
Dallas Times Herald

YOU BETTER HAVE A DARN GOOD REASON FOR PASSING THIS POINT.

John Duncan

TRUE opinion

The following column is reprinted verbatim from the Toronto Sun, *November 12, 1976.*

Body Hygiene
By McKenzie Porter

For more than 40 years I have wanted to write the column that follows. But I have refrained on the grounds of an old fashioned sense of delicacy. Now that general attitudes toward bodily functions are more candid and wholesome I think I may deplore, without being obnoxious, the washroom habits of some men.

The most depressing spectacle a man may see on entering a public washroom to urinate is that of the feet of another man who is seated behind the half-door of a water closet in the act of defecation. There is something wrong with a man who defecates in some washroom outside his home. He is either ill, ignorant or unclean.

The custom of reading the newspaper regularly in a water closet at one's place of employment is not merely a theft of one's employer's time but, often, an offence to the eyes, ears and nose of one's colleagues.

A healthy, intelligent, fastidious man defecates in his home or hotel bathroom in the morning before he takes his shower or tub. In this way he ensures that his body is immaculate before he dons his underwear. Defecation in any place where it is difficult to wash the anus is unhygienic. No matter how good is the quality of the toilet paper available it is never as effective as soap and water.

One of the most impressive ablutionary provisions I ever saw was a latrine for private soldiers of the Indian Army during World War II. Although it was a makeshift affair in range of enemy guns it was equipped with a rudimentary shower made out of old gasoline cans. The private soldiers of this particular regiment, famous for their salubrious appearance, were not content in a latrine with paper. They expected, even in the front line, facilities for washing.

The celebrated freshness of the Indian Army is dependent to a large extent on the regularity of bowel movements. By developing the habit of excreting shortly after arising from sleep, a habit easily acquired by anybody else, the Indian Army soldiers are able to wash conveniently before they dress.

Taking a tip from the Indian Army, many years ago, the British Army introduced the seemingly incongruous barrack-room custom of serving morning tea to soldiers in bed. Such refreshment is called Gunfire. It promotes the routine of morning evacuation, use of the showers and higher standards of cleanliness and health.

Any doctor will tell you that washing with soap and water after excretion is a precaution against minor and major ailments of the rectum.

A common cause of so-called food poisoning is the handling of dishes by restaurant workers who have failed to wash their hands properly after defecation. All staff washrooms in restaurants should be equipped with bidets, or showers, and the use of such, after defecation, should be mandatory.

It is essential, of course, to provide water closets in all places of employment and in public buildings for the use of persons who need them at odd times. But to encourage better habits in the general population each public water closet should carry on its half-door the notice: For Emergency.

On the inside of the door, for the edification of the user, the following notice should be posted: "This Water Closet Is Provided For Persons Suffering From Temporary Irregularity of the Bowels. Healthy Persons Use the Water Closet At Home Where It Is Possible To Wash the Body Before Adjusting the Dress."

Ad from Los Angeles Magazine

TRUE jewelry

TRUE disappointment

TRUE military

Based on a 1970 census report showing the black population of North Dakota as 2,500, the federal government ordered the North Dakota National Guard to recruit 20 blacks.

A study of the recruiting possibilities by the state adjutant general, LeClair A. Melhouse, has revealed, however, that of the 2,500 blacks in the state, all but 150 are airmen or their dependents stationed at an Air Force base near Bismarck.

Of that 150, more than 60 are women; of the remaining 90, only 50 are between the ages of eighteen and forty-five, the statutory limits of military service. Of the 50, 30 are college students, who, in the absence of a draft, are thought to be unlikely to want to interrupt their academic careers to serve in the Guard.

That leaves twenty potential black recruits. Melhouse has accordingly submitted a mandatory black-recruitment plan, which states in its entirety, "If we can find a black, we'll attempt to recruit him."

Washington Post

TRUE government

When James Piepenburg was convicted under Salt Lake City's "obscene performances" ordinance for showing an allegedly pornographic film at his theater, Piepenburg appealed to the Utah Supreme Court. There, Justice A.H. Ellett wrote a majority opinion upholding the lower court, despite the appellant's contention that Salt Lake City's test for obscenity flies in the face of less stringent criteria mandated by the US Supreme Court. Ellett wrote that state judges who subscribe to the US Supreme Court's pornography standards are "depraved, mentally deficient, mind-warped queers."
Idaho State journal

TRUE chores

"Think of yourself as taking out the garbage. Nobody likes to do it, particularly most husbands, who don't like to change diapers either, but imagine what a mess there'd be if no one did. So the job is generally left to the lady of the house. From an article describing proper techniques for removing excess smegma from horse penises.
Horse Woman magazine

TRUE irony

A mobile home owned by Glenn Johnson of Bremerton, Washington, suffered $300 worth of damages from an electrical fire. Fire department investigators traced the source to faulty wiring in Johnson's smoke detector.

AP

TOM SNYDERS, "The Bicycling Comedian," has spent the past seventeen years pedaling his fully loaded touring bicycle to all his stand-up comedy performances. He has cycled more than 124,000 miles throughout 50 states, 11 countries, and three continents. Along the way he snaps pictures of funny signs he encounters on the back roads of the world. He now has a collection of more than 7,000 images—the best of which are featured in this book and in his live performances.

Snyders's car blew up on his way to a comedy performance in 1987. Since then he's been using his bicycle as his main form of transportation. Over the years, he's pedaled onto the set of nine national television shows, including appearances on Comedy Central, ESPN, and *Live with Regis & Kathie Lee*. He's also performed at the best and the worst comedy clubs in the country.

In August 2000 Snyders left Prudhoe Bay, Alaska, on his bike and pedaled the 6,100 miles to Key West, Florida. That would have been a lifetime adventure for anyone else, but for Snyders it was simply an interesting two months within an incredible, ongoing seventeen-year bike trip.

On this journey Snyders has also: been hit by a car and dragged 30 feet; been attacked by a police dog; pedaled up a mountain in the middle of a raging snowstorm; looked a grizzly bear in the eye from 15 feet away; been run out of town by local police in Georgia; and tried to figure out how to possibly have a steady relationship while on the road.

Snyders has written a screenplay; coincidentally, it's about a comedian who travels by bicycle to all his stand-up comedy performances. We don't know how he comes up with this stuff. He bills it as *"Forrest Gump Meets Seabiscuit."*

For more about Snyders and his journey, visit www.bikecomedy.com